BUILDING THE CHURCH
GOD WANTS!

Studies in Church Leadership

Ken Chant

ISBN 978-1-61529-112-0

Vision Publishing
1672 Main St. E 109
Ramona, CA 92065
1-800-9-VISION
www.booksbyvision.com

4

Table of Contents

"Too young a man," *said Blaise Pascal,* "is not a good judge, neither is too old a man." [1]

Since I may fairly claim to be neither one nor the other, my competence to write this book at least remains unimpugned on the ground of age. For the rest, you must decide for yourself; but I hope you will find here some new insights on how to build the church God wants in this last decade of the 20th century. In any case, I am willing to place myself under the same rule as the noble Roman emperor -

"If anyone can show me, and prove to me, that I am wrong in thought or deed, I will gladly change. I seek the truth, which never yet hurt anybody. It is only persistence in self-delusion and ignorance that does harm." [2]

---

[1] Pensées, #58; ed. Louis Lafuma; tr. John Warrington; J. M. Dent & Sons Ltd, London, 1973; pg. 21. Pascal was a 17th century mathematician, scientist, and Christian apologist.

[2] Marcus Aurelius (Roman Emperor A.D. 161-180), Meditations, tr. Maxwell Staniforth; Penguin Books, 1986; Book Six, #21.

AN EASY YOKE

"Come to me, everyone who is weary from carrying a heavy burden, and I will give you rest. Put your neck into my yoke and be taught by me, for then you will find repose for your soul. I am gentle and gracious; my yoke fits well, and my burden is light." [3]

Perhaps no myth is so prevalent in the church as the idea that the ministry is a difficult profession, wearying to the soul and exhausting to the body. That is not how Jesus saw it. He called his yoke *comfortable*, and his burden *light*! The operative word is no doubt *"his"*. The yoke that is easy is *"his"*. The burden that is light is *"his"*. There is nothing in the work *Christ* gives a pastor to do that could ravage him or her emotionally, mentally, physically, or spiritually. The things that destroy us do not come from the Lord's appointment; they arise from the cargoes we either pack ourselves or allow others to stow on us.

When we do what God has called us to do, we have full access to his enabling grace and strength. When we take up extraneous burdens, we are on our own. To carry those loads, we have nothing more to draw upon than personal wisdom and ability. People who labour with such scant resources will surely find their work toilsome, sapping their vitality, wrecking their health, deadening their spirits.

Of course, the gospel does demand from its workers extraordinary sacrifices. The Master's service can bring nakedness, cold, hunger, violence, even death.[4] Yet those sufferings are external to Christian ministry. They are a price we are willing to pay to glorify the name of our God. They may hurt us, but the gospel cannot, for in the task of God itself there is nothing to ulcerate a man's stomach. Preaching Christ cannot block your arteries, or shatter your nerves, or bankrupt your finances! Those disasters are the consequences of things we do outside the divine purpose, carrying burdens God never gave us.

The mistake is common enough, as the following statistics show - [5]

---

[3]   Matthew 11:28-30

[4]   1 Corinthians 4:1; 2 Corinthians 6:4-5; 11:23-28

[5]   I have gleaned these figures from various sources

♦ *In the United States, the average time a pastor remains in the ministry is only six years - which means, of course, that many pastors last only a few months.*

♦ *In Australia a comparable statistic shows that 50% of pastors have abandoned the ministry within five years of their ordination.*

♦ *Ralph Mahoney has said that out of every 100 people called to the ministry, only 10 finally get ordained; and out of that ten only one survives for a lifetime of service.*

♦ *Rowland Croucher has said that in Australia there are about 10,000 clergy serving the various churches, plus another 10,000 who for various reasons have forsaken the ministry.*

Even if those figures are only approximately correct they still represent an appalling tragedy, a measureless loss to the church and to the gospel. Yet those crushed pastors all began their ministry with at least some sense of divine vocation. No one joins the clergy just looking for a job, or even for a career. Almost any other profession offers either better pay or better conditions. Even when men and women enter seminary with no higher goal than to serve humanity, there is still something noble about their choice, some echo of a call of God. Yet five or six years after their ordination, or even less, many pastors find their call dead, their joy dissipated, their love threadbare. Disillusioned, despairing, unhappy, their dream destroyed, they walk away from the pulpit, sometimes also from the church, and sometimes even from Christ.

Even among those who are still serving Christ, there remain pastors for whom the ministry has become arduous, fatiguing drudgery. It drains away their strength, leaving them frustrated, hurt, despondent.

What has gone wrong?

I think we must blame ourselves. We have adopted a false model of ministry, and we have imposed upon each other a set of destructive expectations. This book is an attempt to correct those faults and to offer a positive model for all who want to serve Christ well by building his church in his way.

In this book the scripture translations, unless otherwise noted, are my own. Biblical quotes are printed in italics. Gender specific terms, whenever the context allows, should be taken to include both male and female.

PAUL'S PRESCRIPTION

We should look for a model of Christian ministry that is applicable to every circumstance: bondage or freedom; war or peace; riches or poverty; persecution or applause. A *universally* appropriate model can be the only one that is *biblically* valid. The problem with many current plans is that they presume a peaceful environment, a democratic society, a free, rich, and numerically growing congregation. But Paul gave Timothy a paradigm that can be followed by any group of Christians, large or small, in any situation. It contains four propositions-

> *"Whatever happens, always keep a cool head; put up with hardship; labor to spread the gospel; fulfil all the duties God has given you."*[6]

---

[6]   2 Timothy 4:5

Proposition One:

COOL –

"Whatever happens, always keep a cool head!"

TWO IMPOSTORS

Alfred the Great (849 - c. 900) was among the noblest men who ever occupied a royal throne. A devout Christian, he deeply feared God, and accepted the task of preserving England as a Christian country against hordes of pagan invaders. Winston Churchill penned this majestic portrait of the warrior king -

> "(His) sublime power to rise above the whole force of circumstances, to remain unbiased by the extremes of victory or defeat, to persevere in the teeth of disaster, to greet returning fortune with a cool eye, to have faith in men after repeated betrayals, raises Alfred far above the turmoil of barbaric wars to his pinnacle of deathless glory."[7]

Churchill applied to Alfred a phrase that echoes Paul's instruction to Timothy; he said that the king had learned to *"greet returning fortune with a cool eye"*. Alfred was neither too much depressed by defeat, nor too much elated by triumph; he treated both states as charlatans, and remained calm in all conditions.

That is a lesson we all need to absorb, for what was won yesterday may be lost today; what was lost today, may be won again tomorrow! Who knows what the day will bring? The tides of life flow in and out; the seasons pass impassively through their changing cycles.

Rudyard Kipling expressed the same idea in his famous lines -

> If you can dream - and not make dreams your master;
> If you can think - and not make thoughts your aim;
> If you can meet with triumph and disaster
> And treat those two impostors just the same
> ... You'll be a man my son![8]

---

[7] History of the English Speaking Peoples, Vol 1, Ch 7. Churchill's sonorous description provides a model of Christian character we would all do well to emulate.

[8] From his poem "If". I have quoted the first few lines of the second stanza, plus the last line of the poem.

Recognize those two great impostors: *triumph* and *disaster*. Stay suspicious of both of them. Neither prosperity nor poverty deserve to be the focus of either our joy or our sorrow.

In his personal diary, the excellent Marcus Aurelius:

> "(God) has given us full power not to fall into any of the absolute evils; and if there were real evil in life's other experiences, he would have provided for that too, so that avoidance of it could lie within every man's ability. But when a thing does not worsen the man himself, how can it worsen the life he lives? (God) cannot have been so ignorant as to overlook a hazard of this kind, nor, if aware of it, have been unable to devise a safeguard or a remedy. Neither want of power nor want of skill could have led Nature into the error of allowing good and evil to be visited indiscriminately on the virtuous and sinful alike. Yet living and dying, honor and dishonor, pain and pleasure, riches and poverty, and so forth, are equally the lot of good men and bad. Things like these neither elevate nor degrade; and therefore they are no more good than they are evil."[9]

Marcus Aurelius was writing, of course, from a pagan, not a Christian viewpoint. Yet he echoes the Christian sentiment that nothing can finally worsen a man's *life* unless he allows it to worsen *himself* - which unhappily is just what many people do allow. Because life does not hand them the success it gives to others, they become embittered, angry, and may even turn their back on the call of God. Rather, say both the emperor and the gospel, we should maintain an attitude of unconcern about such things as status, success, prosperity, and the like.

---

[9]   Op. Cit. Bk 2, #11. To the emperor, "God" was more akin to am impersonal (though not wholly uncaring nor indifferent) Creator, than to the Father of Christian revelation.   Aurelius saw God as a wise and presumably benevolent ruler, but hardly more than that. Nonetheless, his words remain true.

> **Prosperity and poverty
> are both scurrilous impostors!**

Riches may increase, but a godly man or woman will not dote on them; and if you are a pastor, that same rule should also govern you. Does your congregation grow ever bigger? Greet it with a cool eye! Does your congregation seem destined to be small? Greet it with a cool eye!

> *"Never fall in love with success, even if your prosperity seems boundless. ... This is what God himself says to everyone who is wise, or strong, or prosperous: never let me hear you boasting about your wisdom, or your valour, or your success! If you must be proud, then confine your pride to this alone: that you know me, and call me your God. Do you understand what delights me on the earth? When I see you doing what I, your Lord, do myself: behaving kindly, doing justly, and living uprightly. Those are the things that bring me pleasure!"[10]*

When a person lives by God's rule, the coming or going of riches (that is, of statistical success or prosperity), will leave him equally untroubled. As Paul said to Timothy, "he will always keep a cool head!" *Other translations put the apostle's instruction this way -*

> *"Always be steady" (RSV)... "Keep steady all the time" (NJB)... "Amid it all, you must keep your head" (BV)... "Whatever happens, be self-possessed" (Moffatt)... "In all things you must remain calm and sane (Way)... "Keep your head in all situations" (NIV) "Keep control of yourself in all circumstances" (GNB).*

Solomon heartily encouraged the same principle -

> *"The discerning person controls his tongue; those who are wise maintain a cool spirit... A person who lacks*

---

[10]   Psalm 62:12; Jeremiah 9:23-24

BUILDING THE CHURCH GOD WANTS!

Studies in Church Leadership

By Ken Chant

> *self control is like a city whose wall is breached; or worse, like one with no wall at all."[11]*

This coolness of eye, this calmness of mind, this sense of proportion, has several applications, beginning with the need to chill one of our worst heats: ambition - *especially when it masquerades as spiritual vision.*

---

[11]   Proverbs 17:27; 25:28

Chapter One:

BIGGER MAY NOT BE BETTER

Have you have been enticed into a misguided admiration of bigness as a thing to be desired above all else? Then meditate upon this -

> "Even the non-religious philosopher and scientist William James has extolled `the little way' in the realm of the natural world. He wrote in a letter to a friend, `As for me, my bed is made. I am against bigness and greatness in all their forms... The bigger the unit you deal with, the hollower, the more brutal, the more mendacious is the life displayed. So I am against all big organisations as such, national ones first and foremost; against all big successes and big results; and in favour of the external forces of truth which always work in an individual and immediately unsuccessful way, underdogs always, till history comes, after they are long dead, and puts them on the top.'"[12]

How far away from that sensible attitude is the habitual admiration this world gives to every kind of material success. The bigger the better! The more the merrier! Let a man amass a few million dollars and even the finest Christian feels obliged to look upon him with awe. Let someone collect an enormous crowd, or create a huge organisation, and no matter how it was done, the world and the church alike hasten to kiss the powerful leader's feet.

In an early 1988 edition of The Times Literary Supplement, Richard Davenport-Hines reviewed a group of books about six business tycoons, who were then all powerful and immensely rich. The books portrayed those men as models of heroic and admirable achievement. Davenport-Hines, however, did not agree -

---

[12]   From an introduction by Dorothy Day to The practice of the Presence of God, by brother Lawrence; Burns & Oates, London, 1977; pg. 18

"These books give a glimpse into the abyss. Their themes are cruelty, hate, and greed; egomaniacs, bullies, liars, blackmailers, wheedlers, toadies, and fools, brawl and swagger through their pages... (They are mostly) morose men gnawed by envy. They pass their days in buying and selling and feuding; they know the price of everything and the value of nothing. They fester with rage, jealousy, enmity, and pride. ... Many of their lives appear sad as well as grotesque.

"It seems necessary, if one wants to be super-rich, to lose touch with most living feelings, and to leave one's family and lovers almost equally deadened or bereft. Several of these financiers regard themselves as gloriously sexy, but the reality is that their most singular achievement has been to make fornication dreary. ...

"No one who reads these accounts of the ravening wolves of cosmopolitan finance can doubt that the system in which they operate is economically ruinous and a pitiful abasement of human values. ... Instead of being the cynosure of admiring eyes... these moguls need to have their financial actions and their human values endlessly and reiteratively denounced. ..." [13]

Not every wealthy person deserves that indictment, nor does every great corporation. It is easy to find many examples of good people who have honorably achieved high renown. But sadly, it is even easier to find corrupt examples which do call for bitter invective. Whether outside the church or inside it, whether in a commercial baron or a church leader, there is something innately defiling about craving for more and more.

Ambition is a most ruinous frenzy

Church history, both ancient and modern, provides countless cases of spiritual nobility broken on the rack of ungodly ambition. Here is one of them, an ancient bishop whose story sounds all too modern! He was immensely popular, he gathered great wealth, he traveled with an

---

[13] Quoted by Martin E Marty, American writer and Christian historian, in the newsletter Context, March 15, 1988

entourage of doting disciples, he encouraged enthusiastic applause, huge crowds flocked to hear him, his morals were suspect, he dressed splendidly, and lived in luxury. His name was Paul of Samosata, and he was bishop of Antioch until a church synod deposed him in the year 272. The outraged dignitaries who exiled him, described him thus -

> "This Paul was formerly poor and beggarly, having inherited not a single possession from his father. But now he has come to have excessive wealth, which he has gained by various means that despoil and oppress the people. He promises to help the injured, for a price, yet deceives them all the while; for he takes advantage of the readiness to give that people have when they are in difficulty, because they hope to be delivered from whatever is troubling them. He thus supposes that monetary gain is godliness.

> "How can I describe his pride, and the haughtiness with which he has assumed worldly dignities? He struts through the market-place, escorted by multitudes of people who go both before him and after him.[14] I am ashamed to tell of the quackery he practices in the ecclesiastical assemblies, by which he courts popularity, making a great parade, and astounding by his arts the minds of the less sophisticated. He also sets up for himself a lofty tribunal and throne, after the manner of the rulers of this world, and he then censures and insults those who do not applaud him nor wave their handkerchiefs at him, while bawling aloud and leaping about.

> "Those who sing his praise and eulogize him among the people declare that their impious teacher has come down as an angel from heaven, but the haughty man makes no effort to check such utterances. Then again, there are the groups of women who attend him,[15] and who are supported by him and by the presbyters and deacons

---

[14] The reference is to groups of retainers and bodyguards.

[15] Groups of priests, housekeepers and deaconesses. No charge of actual immorality was ever proved against Paul or his associates.

with him. Besides this, he has made his followers rich, and for that he is loved and admired by those who set their hearts upon such things.

"After such behavior, how can he now censure another man, or warn him to beware of yielding to greater familiarity with a woman, lest perchance he might slip? For although Paul has dismissed one of the women who were with him, he has still retained two others, and these are in the bloom of their youth, and of fair countenance. When he goes away, he actually takes them with him, all the while indulging in luxury and surfeiting."[16]

How familiar that description sounds! How sad that a man with such powerful gifts should have sacrificed them on the altar of success. He was not the first to do so, nor the last.

> **Envy of bigness is a deadly poison.**

From a real person in the 3rd century we can jump to a fictional character in the 20th, and hear the same wisdom. A young lady approached the great detective, Charlie Chan, and asked him if he were ambitious -

"Chan turned to her gravely. `Coarse food to eat, water to drink, and the bended arm for a pillow - that is an old definition of happiness in my country. What is ambition? A canker that eats at the heart of the (driven) man, denying him the joys of contentment.'"[17]

What God builds, in fulfillment of his divine purpose, whether it is large or small, retains the character of holiness; what a man builds, driven by ambition, no matter how successful it may seem outwardly, lies in the shadow of death.

Admiration of bigness, and worse, envy of it, are truly a deadly poison. We who preach against covetousness may ourselves be deeply guilty of

---

[16] Based on the "Letter of Malchion;" Anti-Nicene Fathers Vol. 6; tr. by A. Cleveland Coxe; 1978 reprint of the 19th century work; Eerdmans Pub. Co; pg. 169,170

[17] Behind the Curtain, by E. D. Biggers; Bantam Books, New York, 1974; pg 16

it. Are you a pastor? You may not yearn for your neighbor's wife, but are you any better than an adulterer if you crave his church?

Of course, we disguise our ugly greed by such pious dissembling as "godly envy... holy ambition... inspired vision... earnest zeal," and the like. Alas! we delude only ourselves. God is not deceived, and our carnal desires, full of self aggrandizement, hungry for prestige, longing for power, attract only his scorn. Worn down by toil, emotionally exhausted, spiritually vitiated, we are fortunate indeed if we learn humility and contentment in time to save us from the full consequences of our folly!

Have you ever thought about this? The last and most powerful temptation Satan thrust upon the starving Jesus in the desert was an appeal to *ambition*[18]. The story raises a question: is it ever possible for a person to get possession of the wealth, honor, praise, or rule of this world (in the church or out of it), without somehow bowing before the devil?

Why is this?

Simply because the benefits of bigness usually come only at terrible cost.

For example: in the ancient world, around the time of Paul, the empire of Rome, stretching from the western shores of Europe to the eastern bounds of Asia Minor, brought unprecedented prosperity to its 200 million citizens. Wherever the rule of Caesar prevailed there was good order, safe travel by land or sea, a common law and culture, liberty to pursue whatever vocation one pleased, the finest civilization the world had ever known.

The grateful multitude of the emperor's subjects, who for centuries had suffered endless wars and the depredations of countless tyrants, great and small, reveled in the *Pax Romana* and gratefully called *Caesar the "Savior of the World"*.[19]

Yet behind the facade of peace there remained a ruthless tyranny, which brooked not the slightest opposition; and underlying the empire's

---

[18] Matthew 4:8

[19] Which gives special force to the NT use of Saviour as a title for Christ, especially in connection with his role as King of kings (Luke 2:11; Philippians 3:20; 1 Timothy 4:10; 2 Peter 1:11; 1 John 4:14; etc.

glittering success was a foundation of corpses, the bodies of millions whose slaughter alone gave Caesar his triumph.

Has it ever been any different? What empire has ever been built and maintained without enormous cost in human life? Ask the thousands of Scots, Welsh, and Irish, the tens of thousands of brown, black, red, and yellow natives who perished during the years England was expanding her dominion, whether the benefit of empire was worth the misery it caused! Can such enlargement, whether commercial or political, be achieved without oppression and violence? Usually, the answer must be, "No!"

Thus a hundred years ago Oscar Wilde, in his poem Ave Imperatrix, spoke about the shame of the countless dead whose lives were the cost of England's imperial ambition. The pomp and glory cast a dark shadow; the shouts of triumph hid the sound of bitter grief -

> "What profit now that we have bound
> The whole world round with nets of gold,
> If hidden in our heart is found
> The care that groweth never old?"[20]

Similarly, in Ben Jonson's 17th. century play Sejanus, Tiberius Caesar learnt that his power rested upon tyranny. The emperor was taught this lesson by his chief adviser, Sejanus, who warned Tiberius not to be dismayed by the hatred of his subjects -

> Sejanus: Whom hatred frights,
>   Let him not dream of sovereignty.
> Tiberius: Are rights
>   Of faith, love, piety, to be trod down,
>   Forgotten, and made vain?
> Sejanus: All for a crown.
>   The prince who shames a tyrant's name to bear
>   Shall never do anything, but fear;
>   All the command of scepters quite doth perish,
>   If they begin religious thoughts to cherish... "

The same is true of Christian "empires"; that is, something of the tyrant's spirit is present in any leader who is determined to make his "kingdom"

---

[20]   Stanza 26

bigger and bigger. It seems impossible for any man who aspires to excessive success to reach his goal without accepting some measure of corruption. Nor can he do it without some willingness to crush and discard anyone who impedes his progress.

The single exception to this rule - that empires cannot be built without squandering life - is found in the true kingdom of God. Among all dominions this one alone has established its world-wide reign, not upon organizational ruthlessness, but upon a cross. Its chief dynamic is not earthly success, but self-denying love. It grows, not by taking life, but by giving it.

Yet even Jesus was tempted to build his kingdom another way - to capture the nations of this world and all their glory by falling in worship before the devil. But he refused to be tempted by the prospect of an easy triumph. Instead, he resolutely turned his face toward Calvary, pursued the pathway of self-denial, and thus established the greatest kingdom the world will ever know - and the only one that is eternally indestructible!

Chapter Two:

THE TENTH COMMANDMENT

There is a good reason why the sages have consistently preferred smallness to bigness. It is this: when the great fall, they ruin thousands; but if a small man falls, he harms only himself. Sadly, the great often fall, because there are many among them who know how to take a walled city, but cannot rule their own spirits.[21] In the end, as Solomon said, the bravest deed any of us can accomplish is to gain mastery over ourselves.

A story is told of the North African Muslim saint, the sheik al-Alawi (1869-1934). He once challenged a famous snake-charmer to control a viper more venomous than any he had before handled. The magician, indignant, yet anxious also to impress the holy man, demanded to be shown the snake he could not bend to his will. The sheik told him that the serpent the charmer could not subdue was the man's own soul. If the fakir could conquer his soul as well as he did his reptiles, then his claim to fame would be unshakable.[22]

When the great fall, they ruin thousands.

Moved by the same idea, Charles Kingsley put these words into the mouth of the great Elizabethan sea captain, Sir Richard Grenville -

> "To be bold against the enemy is common to the brute; but the prerogative of a man is to be bold against himself. ... To conquer our own fancies, (and) our own lusts, and our ambition, in the sacred name of duty; this is to be truly brave, and truly strong; for he who cannot rule himself, how can he rule his crew or his fortunes?"[23]

---

[21] Proverbs 16:32

[22] I adapted this story from an article by Lamin Sanneh in Christian Century magazine, Apr 10, 1991; pg 399.

[23] Westward Ho!, Chap. One.

Another renowned Elizabethan, Sir Walter Raleigh, is also one of the characters in Kingsley's novel. At one point he is in Ireland, discussing with a friend a noble plan to civilise the (then) barbarous Irish, and to turn the wilderness into fertile fields. Raleigh is speaking, questioning to himself whether his motives are as pure as he imagines, or whether he can (when so many others have failed) withstand the corruptions of fame and power -

> "What wilt thou be when thou hast (thy heart's desire)? Will thy children sink downwards, as these noble barons sank? Will the genius of tyranny and falsehood find soil within thy heart to grow and ripen fruit? What guarantee hast thou for doing better here than those who went before thee?... But - here, away from courts, among a people who should bless me as their benefactor and deliverer - what golden days might be mine! And yet - is this but another angel's mask from that same cunning fiend Ambition's stage? And will my house be indeed the house of God, the foundations of which are loyalty, and its bulwarks righteousness, and not the house of Fame, whose walls are of the soap-bubble...? I would be good and great - when will the day come when I shall be content to be good, and yet not great...? Greatness? I have tasted that cup...; do I not know that it is sweet in the mouth, but bitter in the belly?"[24]

Craving another man's church

breaks the Tenth Commandment.

So again I ask: why would a man of God hunger for greatness? You may reply: "Surely *God* wants me to do great things, to fly high, to build a superb church, to gather a congregation of hundreds, if not thousands?" Perhaps; but equally, perhaps not. Neither scripture nor life gives any indication that God calls ordinary people to do more than ordinary things. Very few are equipped to rise above a normal level of achievement. Most of us have to be content with humble aspirations.

---

[24]   Ibid Ch. 11

Of course you, my reader, *may* be one of those few; yet still you should beware. The greater the height the further to fall. The more visible the target, the easier to strike it. The larger the fortune, the more it will attract hungry thieves. The scandals blazoned in endless headlines show the perils that may beset the famous, both inside and outside the church.

Undoubtedly we *should* strive to be as great as God desires us to become, and to achieve as much as he will permit. Scripture shows clearly enough that whatever part of God's purpose we fail to complete will be a matter for judgment at the bench of Christ.[25] So we had better labor to realize our maximum potential.

Nonetheless, the opposite idea is just as true: we should be satisfied to be or to do as *little* as God has decreed. There is no virtue in trying to do *more* than the Lord has commanded, nor in struggling to be *more* than he has made us to be.[26] It is enough for each of us simply to fulfil the Father's plan for our lives, whether that confines us to comparative obscurity, or carries us to astonishing renown. Now that is a pious sentiment. But even while we "amen" it, our ambitions war against it fiercely. How mightily our vaunting pride resists crucifixion! Our entire society lives by the axiom that greatness is the only acceptable aspiration. It seems almost blasphemous to suggest that we might more sensibly delight in a modest estate; yet the wise have always commended humility.

More than three hundred years ago, Blaise Pascal made a similar observation -

> "How extraordinary it is that so evident a fact as the vanity of the world is so little recognised that we think it strange and surprising to say that the search for greatness is folly."[27]

History is full of stories about people who found only sorrow when they tried to fly too high or do too much. To be born to greatness, or to have

---

[25] See 1 Corinthians 3:10-15; etc

[26] Note that this was the peculiar fault of Nadab and Abihu (Leviticus 10:1-3): "they offered before the Lord unauthorized fire, which he had not commanded them to offer." Their fault was not in doing what God had forbidden, but rather in doing what he had not commanded.

[27] Pensees #53; op. cit. Pg. 21

greatness spring on one unaware, may be safe. But has there ever been a case of one who has deliberately sought greatness and not found its sparkling wine spiked with poison?

Cool those heated passions!

Just as you do, so I too yearn to live as nobly, richly, productively, as I can. Who could accept any lesser goal in life? Yet neither can I deny that there is something inherently perilous in aching to be successful - especially if "success" is defined only as visible or statistical achievement. Paul had a better focus -

> *"Of course, I have not already reached my goal, nor am I already perfect; but I intend to press on until I have seized everything for which Christ seized me. Dear friends, I dare not claim to have grasped all of it yet; but you can be sure of this: forgetting what is behind me, and pressing on to what lies ahead, I am striving to run the race well, right to the very end of the track. My aim is to win the prize of the heavenly call of God in Christ Jesus. If you think yourself mature, you should embrace the same ambition!"[28]*

We always claim, of course, that we are pursuing a spiritual (not a worldly) goal; yet in the end we measure success by the same fiscal and statistical criteria that rule the world. We tend to crave the status symbols our ungodly neighbors admire, as the outward marks of our triumphs: a big house, a fine car, a large income, a splendid church building, and the like. We reckon that such things are the proofs of divine favor. But if so, by whose favor do the wicked amass their wealth?

Where then is your eye truly fixed? On earth or heaven? On the worldly prize of fame, or the spiritual reward of Christ? Give an honest answer, otherwise you will rob only yourself. Whoever has thought soberly about these issues has come to the same conclusion, and warned the compulsive adventurer -

---

[28] Philippians 3:12-15

Rash dreamer, return. O, ye winds of the main,
Bear him back to his own peaceful Ara again.
Rash fool! for a vision of fanciful bliss,
To barter thy calm life of labor and peace.
The warning of reason was spoken in vain;
He never re-visited Ara again!
Night fell on the deep, amidst tempest and spray,
And he died on the waters, away, far away![29]

How then should we think? What should we do? Firstly keep a cool head! Then press on to the best, the highest, the richest, we can obtain under the hand of God. If the Lord gives you grand success, think little of it. Christ is the prize you are seeking, not human renown. If the fruit of your labors is scant, what does it matter? You have won Christ, and there is no higher goal!

---

[29] From Gerald Griffins poems Hy-Brassail, last stanza. "Ara" was the homeland of the mariner, who despised its quiet wealth of love, and sailed off in quest of a magical land of glittering fortune.

Chapter Three:

WHAT IS "SUCCESS"?

The idea has been promulgated that the pastor's main task is to grow the church numerically, and that true success in ministry must be measured by statistical increase. Has there ever been a sadder doctrine adopted by the church? The impious ambitions that underlie such notions have left the nation strewn with the wreckage of once devout servants of God.

So continuing from our previous chapter, if you are a church leader, let me ask again: what *is* your proper goal? To build a *big* church? To build a *small* church? Or is it simply to build the church God wants, and leave the size of it in his hands?

Let us examine the options.

Big churches are wonderful!

Who can doubt the immense value of large churches? Among their benefits we could list the following, and much more:

♦ *they make a powerful impact on the community*

♦ *they speak with a national voice*

♦ *they have resources to do things in evangelism, missionary outreach, use of the media, etc, far beyond the capacity of smaller congregations.*

But everything has its price. That is a principle of life. Nothing is accomplished without cost, and the cost of a big church is high indeed. So before you too easily assume that God has called you to build a large and flourishing congregation, consider whether you can afford it. You may find it too expensive - far outside the limit of your personal resources - to advance from where you are and into the leadership of a much larger church.

Am I talking about money? Of course not, but about the emotional and spiritual cost that a rapidly growing church may exact from you.

What is that cost? Here are some things you must consider, some issues or changes you must face. Church leaders should ask themselves if they are willing, or able, to pay the price of

1. PRAGMATISM

The builder and leader of a large church must be able to move away from a gentle piety into an aggressive pursuit of growth. That is a change which for many pastors is simply impossible. It marks two different temperaments, two different leadership styles. Neither one is better than the other - they are just different. An illustration of these two contrasting approaches to the service of God can be found in Ezra and Nehemiah: the one pious; the other pragmatic.

Ezra was mystical in character, a man of prayer, and deeply immersed in scripture. A suggestion that he should depend for protection upon a military escort scandalized him;[30] he preferred to trust God for safety. When he saw the sin of the people, he wept bitterly for hours, fasted, clothed himself in sackcloth, and poured ashes over his head.

Nehemiah had an opposite temperament. He was a man of action, and he rode into Jerusalem at the head of a glittering military escort.[31] All his dealings were marked by shrewdness; he reacted furiously against sin; he sternly punished wrongdoers; he could not depend upon prayer alone, but armed the people with swords.

Someone has said that when the people sinned, Ezra pulled out his own hair and beat *himself*, while Nehemiah beat the *sinners* and pulled out their hair!

Ezra did what Nehemiah could not: he established a new nation around the scriptures and Israel's covenant with God. *Nehemiah* did what Ezra could not: he built the walls of Jerusalem and set up an effective civil administration. Ezra was the private man of learning, and the teacher of the people; while Nehemiah was the man of public affairs, the commander of the nation. Yet scripture gives equal praise to both men.[32]

---

[30] Ezra 8:21-22
[31] Nehemiah 2:9b
[32] Consider the inference of Nehemiah 12:26b

The kingdom of God needs both kinds of servants; both have their proper work. But if you are an "Ezra", you cannot emulate a "Nehemiah"; and vice versa. Each of us must find our own true nature, and work in conformity with what we are, not what we might want to be. And the usual rule is that those with a "Nehemiah" temperament can far more easily gather and manage a large congregation than those can who have an "Ezra" temperament.

2. TRANSFERENCE

A point comes in the life of any growing congregation when a crossover must be made from a "family" to a "corporate" model of the church. This requires the adoption of a different set of organizational dynamics - the same kind of difference that lies between an ordinary family and a business corporation. Both entities need structure and rules; they require good management of their resources; they depend upon harmonious inter-personal relationships. Nonetheless, the way a loving father runs his family differs radically from the way an efficient manager runs a business. One is motivated by affection, mutual dependence, and permanency; the other is ruled by productivity, dividends, and a constant change of personnel. Some of those same differences inescapably exist between the structural identity of small and large churches.

So, beyond a certain level, a growing church must begin to adopt an increasingly secular methodology. In the end there may be no significant difference between the structure, staffing, and running of that church and the style of the prosperous commercial enterprise around the corner. Some pastors thrive in that environment; others are crushed by it.

> **Do you have a "rancher" or a "shepherd" mentality?**

Another way to express it is to think about shifting from a "shepherd" to a "rancher" mentality. The true shepherd (in biblical imagery) knows each sheep by name, and cares for them individually; his sheep are at least as important to him for their sake as they might be for any profit he hopes to gain from them. But a modern rancher, numbering his sheep in thousands, cares little for the individual sheep; his eye is on the profitability of his flock as a whole.

Similarly, the consuming interest of the pastor of a large church cannot be the single member; he must focus rather upon the whole flock. But for most pastors, that loss of personal involvement with each of the people is too high a price to pay for mere growth. So the average pastor may yearn in one part of his mind for his congregation to multiply hugely, but another (and more dominant) part of his nature constantly prevents it from happening.

Depending upon what God has called a pastor to do, this "transference" we are examining could be for him either godly or ungodly. For some these steps are right; for others they are wrong. But in either case, if a congregation keeps on growing numerically, they will become necessary. There is no other way for that church to build increasing success in marketing its product. You must ask yourself whether you can make such transitions. Few men and women can do so. Most pastors find them emotionally and spiritually impossible. The cost they exact is too personally ravaging.

3. STRUCTURE

As a local church family turns into a large and prosperous organization, reliance upon informal spiritual authority alone has to be replaced by something more akin to a secular power structure. That is, the church is forced ever closer to the command pattern of a normal commercial enterprise. Inescapably it is drawn away from the biblical model of a living "Body" controlled by the "Head", Jesus Christ. It changes from an intimate *organism* into a largely impersonal *organization*.

Is that what you want for your congregation? Could you tolerate such changes if they were to happen? Has God really called and equipped you to run a corporation; or are you better fitted to guide a family? Do you match the job description of a sheep station manager, or that of a biblical shepherd? An honest response to those questions will draw from some pastors a "Yes!", for the driving force of their ministry is to build the church bigger and bigger. From others, the only possible response will be "No!", for their deepest aspirations cannot be fulfilled simply by expanding the size of their congregation. If you are a pastor, you must find your own answer.

4. MANAGEMENT

Pastors of large churches must possess both the willingness and the ability to motivate their staff, and to control them. Great leaders are able to inspire in their assistants a deep loyalty and a compliant subjugation of their personal ambitions to the goals of the leader. Such pastors must also be able to fire personnel as readily as they can hire them. Successful managers know how to set and how to enforce standards of efficiency, diligence, and production.

Few men and women have such a package of capabilities - which is why those in the secular world who do possess them draw such enormous salaries. If you lack those skills, then your dream of a large congregation is in reality a nightmare that will destroy you if you pursue it. You should adopt more modest goals.

5. DISCIPLINE

In order to gain the many benefits created by a big church, its leaders must relax other demands. For example: how is it possible for people in a large assembly to forge a covenant relationship with each other, bonded together by love, living holy lives under the lordship of Christ? Big congregations require a non-confrontational style, in which the pastors must tolerate in their people a lower level of spirituality and commitment.

Can you adjust to the necessity of a more casual discipline for the sake of keeping attendance at maximum level? Can you accept the pressure of keeping the numerical graph rising, because otherwise the financial security of the church might be threatened? Can you endure a congregation made up mostly of "hearers" rather than "doers" of the word of God? If not, you will never pastor a large church.

For some pastors, the loss of congregational discipline, maturity, and the like, seems a small price for the worth of an immense congregation. But for others, the cost of prolific growth is the impossible one of destroying their deepest commitments. They have to accept that they will never gather nor shepherd pastor a numerous flock.

6. COHESIVENESS

The *koinonia* that was among the chief glories of the early church becomes diluted in a large congregation, where the people are mostly strangers to each other. Although home fellowships may partially replace this loss, they remain an admission that the church itself is no longer a place of true cohesion. Firm loyalty, warm friendship, blended worship, and indestructible unity, are all weakened. The church may be big, but it is now also fragile, more easily destroyed, highly vulnerable. The assembled people are now not so much a congregation as they are an audience.

Exciting, influential, powerful as a big church may be, I think smaller congregations retain a stronger possibility of expressing the biblical qualities of a true church. It seems to me that as a congregation grows larger, two things begin to happen: *first*, it must move ever further away from the scriptural pattern of a local church; and *second*, it must more and more replace the special dynamics of the kingdom of God with an increasingly secular dynamic.

Does that throw big churches out of the kingdom of God? Of course not! The Lord obviously raises up gifted leaders to build huge churches, and how can we do other than rejoice in what God has wrought? Such churches have an important function in the divine economy; they do things that otherwise would not be done. So I love a big church. But I prefer a smaller one. A congregation of, say, two *hundred*,[33] rather than one of two *thousand*, seems to me more likely to maintain all the qualities the New Testament ascribes to a true church.

> **I am not opposing big churches, but affirming small ones.**

Does that sound inconsistent, even self-contradictory? I am sure it does; but there are many anomalies in the kingdom! Everywhere in scripture a tension exists between self-canceling statements, ideas that deeply qualify each other.[34] The Lord has delighted in creating a kingdom, both

---

[33] Not an altogether arbitrary figure. Surveys have shown that a majority of people, if given a viable option, would choose to worship in a church numbering about two hundred. It is large enough to provide a full range of activities but small enough to keep a family identity.

[34] Consider the degree of hyperbole in the following verses: Proverbs 22:29 (compared with Ecclesiastes 9:11); Proverbs 12:21 (compared with say, the story of Job); Proverbs 18:22 (compared with 21:9); Proverbs 22:6 (compared with 17:25). See also Mark 9:43-47 and other equally stunning passages that we don't hesitate to modify severely. Then there are the promises of prosperity, opposed by the injunction to embrace poverty; the promises of victory, opposed by warnings of imprisonment; promises of joy opposed by the certainty of tears; promises of strength, opposed by declarations of weakness; promises of success, opposed by anticipations of barrenness and so on.

natural and spiritual, in which riddles and mysteries abound! To demand absolute uniformity and agreement in doctrine is to demand the ridiculous, for there is no such thing in scripture or in life. As Ralph Waldo Emerson said -

> "A foolish consistency is the hobgoblin of little minds, adored by little statesmen and philosophers and divines. With consistency a great soul has simply nothing to do. ... Speak what you think today in hard words, and tomorrow speak what tomorrow thinks in hard words again, though it contradicts everything you said today."[35]

So I have no qualms about saying that big churches are from God, while continuing to think that small churches are more biblical (or at least, more normal).

Why then this book? *First*, because there is a need to call all churches (large and small) to reflect more brightly the principles of scripture; and *second*, to take up the case for the smaller church. Megachurches don't need an apologist; they are their own best justification! Nor do they need another book, telling how to build one. The saturated market already staggers under an excessive burden of church growth literature. But too many pastors have been misled into believing that anyone who uses the right technique can produce unending congregational growth. That is a delusion I am trying to undo. Let it be spoken loudly: *in reality few pastors can tolerate the cost of crossover from a small to a large church.*

You may of course be someone whom God *has* called to go out and do extraordinary exploits for him. You may be a capable, inspiring, single-minded, visionary, bold, leader who is destined to gather an enormous crowd together. If so, I pray that the great church you build will shine like a beacon in the darkness, and become a haven for a multitude of souls. Whatever the price may be, God has made you both *willing* and *able* to meet every demand.

Yet for most people, to pay such a price merely for statistical success is too high. Not because they are *unwilling* to pay it; but because they are *incapable* of doing so. If you are one of those more average pastors, then you have no choice except to be content with humbler aspirations, and to

---

[35] Essays: First Series; "Self Reliance" (1841).

devote your life to shepherding a church of modest size. But what is wrong with that? Is it not a joyful and splendidly rewarding task. For indeed, if big churches are wonderful (and they are), then small churches are at least equally wonderful!

That is the theme of the next chapter.

Chapter Four:

AFFIRMING SMALL CHURCHES

Were there some practical way to do so, I would abandon the terminology "big" and "small", for it is misleading. It creates a false tension. It suggests that one is better than the other, or that one pastor has failed while another has succeeded. Yet there is only one "success", and that is for each pastor to build and shepherd the church God wants, whether it is numerically small or large. However, since so many have said so much in our time about church growth, and they have put so much pressure upon pastors to measure their success by constant statistical increase, I want to argue for a different model of the church and of the ministry.

Small churches are wonderful!

Call this, if you like, a protest against the church growth movement, or at least against that distortion of it which says that big is better, and that small is failure. Call this a cry for a return to a humble and godly concept of the pastor's role. False expectations have shredded too many good people. Crushed by demands they cannot fulfil, they lapse into a dispirited torpor, or abandon the ministry altogether.

Write this indelibly: *the Lord's yoke is easy; the Master's burden is light!* There is nothing in it that could destroy any Christian. On the contrary, the true call of Christ brings with it a constantly renewing vitality, an ever fresh excitement. It is a never-ending source of flowing joy and measureless satisfaction. No ulcers there! No heart attacks or nervous exhaustion! No mental collapse nor emotional or moral ruin! No decay of vision nor waning of vocation! Only rising zeal, and strength more than sufficient for each new demand!

If the ministry of the gospel has destroyed or is threatening to destroy you, then one of two things must be true: *either you are carrying a burden the Lord never gave you to carry*; or, *you are carrying the right burden in the wrong way.* Both faults have wrought tragic consequences.

It is better to discover the task God has given you to do, and to fulfil it in the way he has ordained. How can you do that?

When Jesus described the ideal shepherd and his sheep, is it just a coincidence that the flock numbered one hundred? In Bible days that was a large enough flock to support a shepherd and his family comfortably, but small enough for the shepherd to name and to know each sheep personally. Indeed the ideal shepherd was unwilling to lose even one sheep from his flock. It was not too much for him to risk his life for his sheep.[36] How different that is from the "rancher" mentality of our time (both on the farm and in the church), where the sheep may instead be expected to risk *their* lives for the shepherd!

> ## Let God build each church as big as he wants to build it

Just as a prosperous flock in Bible days numbered about a hundred sheep, so the average church in our day numbers about a hundred people.[37] If a pastor has a Sunday morning congregation of more than one hundred he stands among the top 35% of achievers in church life - which in any other field would be reckoned a successful accomplishment. He has no reason to think himself a failure.

What should we do then? Simply let God build each local church as big as he wants to build it. Or, if you prefer to grieve the Lord, do this: either refuse to do as much as God commands; or resolve to do more than God commands. Both faults are equally ungodly.

So let no one foolishly try to limit God, nor put a ceiling on how large a church can grow. I suppose, even in this age of megachurches, we have not yet seen the biggest congregation God intends to build! Who would want to stop God? Let us watch with joy whatever the Lord pleases to do.

But the opposite is equally true: let no one irresponsibly try to push a church, or a pastor, beyond the limits God has appointed. And since the average congregation is about a hundred strong, and since most pastors are average people with average skills, most of us must learn to be

---

[36] Luke 15:3-7; John 10:3-4, 11, 14

[37] Indeed, throughout the history of the church, the average congregation, pastored by one man, has remained about a hundred strong

content with the average. All the wishing and working in the world cannot turn a normal church with a normal pastor into a megachurch, or even one significantly larger than it is already.

Yet why should that be thought shameful? Even on the crassest level of money, a congregation of a hundred or so people (like the Biblical flock of a hundred sheep) is adequate to meet the financial needs of the shepherd and his family. He may not be rich, but he will have all that he needs. Why should a Christian want more? Since when did gathering wealth become a proper goal for the servant of God?

Further, if a pastor truly gives himself (or herself) to the care of the sheep, and to ensuring that none of them strays from the kingdom of God, even an average flock of a hundred or so will provide enough work for a lifetime of fulfilling ministry.

> **Since when were riches**
>
> **a proper goal for the servant of God?**

Do I mean that growth is no longer important? Hardly! Every church must have a goal for growth; but, (as I shall show later) one of the best ways to create that growth is to plant more churches. The most effective plan ever devised to evangelise a community is to establish a local church there! The main reason for any church to exist is to plant another, and then another, and then another!

Let me ask again: how big should a church be? As big as you and God can make it! But keep on reminding yourself of this: as surely as a pastor, without God's help, can keep his (or her) church smaller than God wants it, so, still without God's help, he can make it bigger than God wants it! But whether a church is big or small, still its *major* thrust ought not to be getting bigger and fatter, but rather expansion by planting other churches.

> **Is he talking only to shopkeepers, or also to pastors?**

Jesus gave a warning to those who enjoy unusual success in their earthly activities -

"How hard it is for a rich man to enter the kingdom of God! Therefore, do not live for money; instead, be content with what you have". [38]

Was he talking only about money? Or is "money" a synonym for any craving to be reckoned "successful" by the world? Does it apply only to a shopkeeper who is frustrated by his inability to enlarge his business? Or does it rebuke also the pastor who is aggravated by his inability to grow his church? We must learn to be content with what we have! Even if riches (or our congregations) increase, those who are wise will not set their hearts upon them.[39] A godly character is shown by willingness to accept cheerfully whatever favour God has shown. The humble servant happily occupies whatever place the Master assigns.

One of the finest Christians in the annals of the English church was the 17th century physician, Sir Thomas Browne.[40] Despite living during a tempestuous time of intolerance and religious persecution, constantly surrounded by bigotry and violence, his kindness toward all people never failed. During his own lifetime his various books sold out several editions, and have never been out of print across the past 300 years. Let him now speak again, with some wise words on divine providence -

---

There is a time to advance, and a time to withdraw

"Guide not the Hand of God, nor order the Finger of the Almighty unto thy will and pleasure; but sit quiet in the soft showers of Providence, and Favourable distributions in this World, either to thyself or others. And since not only Judgments have their Errands, but Mercies their Commissions, snatch not at every Favour, nor think thyself passed by, if they fall upon thy Neighbour.

"Rake not up envious displacences[41] at things successful unto others, which the wise Disposer of all things thinks not fit for thyself. Reconcile the events of things unto both

---

[38] Mark 10:25; Hebrews 13:15

[39] Psalm 62:10

[40] He was born in 1605 and died 77 years later.

[41] Displeasure's about

beings, that is, of this World and the Next: so will there not seem so many Riddles in Providence, nor various inequalities in the dispensation of things below. ...

"Court not Felicity too far, and weary not the favourable hand of Fortune. Glorious actions have their times, extent, and (limits). To put no end unto Attempts were to make prescriptions of Successes,[42] and to bespeak unhappiness at the last. For the Line of our Lives is drawn with white and black vicissitudes, wherein the extremes hold seldom one complexion. That Pompey *should obtain the sirname of Great at twentyfive years, that Men in their young and active days should be fortunate and perform notable things, is no observation of deep wonder, they having the strength of their fates before them.* ...

"And therefore many brave men finding their fortune grow faint, and feeling its declination, have timely withdrawn themselves from great attempts, and so escaped the ends of Mighty men, disproportionate to their beginnings. But magnanimous Thoughts have so dimmed the eyes of many, that, forgetting the very essence of Fortune, and the vicissitudes of good and evil, they apprehend no bottom in felicity; and so have been still tempted on unto mighty Actions, reserved for their destruction."[43]

Whether young or old, it is a wise person indeed who knows when to advance toward "great attempts" and when to withdraw from them. Unhappily, what Sir Thomas called "magnanimous thoughts" (which we might call "positive thinking") has "dimmed the eyes of many", who press on along the path of fools, never allowing that any misfortune or failure can ever catch them, never doubting that God must always want

---

[42] How many there are today who try to do just that: "make prescriptions out of successes". That is, they try to reduce success to a formula, a method, a set of rules. No doubt there are worse ways than wrong ways to do things but in the end, how much any of us can achieve in life (or in Ministry), rests in a providence beyond our control. The result of an unfounded expectation, of insisting upon unbroken increase (as Sir Thomas said), is likely to be a harvest of unhappiness.

[43] Sir Thomas Browne: The major works, ed. By C. A. Patrides; "Christian morals", Part III.5 and Part II.10

them to attain ever higher pinnacles of "success". That is a "prescription", not for triumph, but more likely for grief.

See how little God is impressed by what this world (and much of the church) admires -

> *"Never forget, dear friends, what kind of people you were when God called you. Not many of you were reckoned wise by this world, not many of you had any power or could boast of high birth. That is because God wanted to shame those who think they are wise by choosing 'fools', and to discomfort those who think they strong by choosing the 'weak'. So he picked you, low and despised in this world though you were - mere nobodies - to make a mockery of the world's way of doing things. In this way, God has left nowhere for human pride to stand in his presence."[44]*

Notice that God *does* call *some* who are wise, and high born, noble and rich; which is to say, he does raise *some* churches to be prolific and powerful, and gives them superbly gifted leaders. Yet not often. Otherwise people might forget that *the excellency of the power* that is revealed in the church - humble though it may be, like a battered clay pot - *comes from God, and not from us.*[45]

We need then to learn how to set reasonable goals - neither less nor more than the Lord himself desires.

Holy aspirations may be only a pious subterfuge

Enthusiastic people are prone to make bold pronouncements about the mighty church they intend to build, or the superb work they intend to do. Others go around "claiming the city" or even the "nation" for Christ. They sing brave songs about the land belonging to Christ; they proclaim the certainty of coming national "revival"; they declare that a vast harvest of souls is on the verge of being reaped.

---

[44] 1 Corinthians 1:26-29

[45] 2 Corinthians 4:7

Who could hope for anything less? May their songs, their prayers, their faith confessions, be wonderfully fulfilled! But the aspirations they express are not realistic, and may in the end be little more than a pious subterfuge, hiding error or unbelief behind a camouflage of heroic claims. In the confident proclamation of national revival, widely heard among charismatic churches, I see several problems -

First: it is unbiblical. Except in an ultimate sense the nation does not and never has belonged to Christ.

For the present time, the citizens of our land have deliberately sold themselves to the devil, and willingly remain his servants. Therefore scripture says, *"the whole world is under the control of the Wicked One";* and that Satan is *"the prince of this world."* He has power to give to whomever he pleases *"all the kingdoms of this world, and their glory";* and the like.[46]

In other words, for now only the Church belongs to Christ; the world still lies in the grip of the Enemy. Calvary actually provides salvation only to those who belong to the church. For the rest of humanity, the cross is a symbol, not of mercy, but of the wrath of the Almighty against sin, and of his coming judgment. Remember that Jesus himself predicted, not vast revivals sweeping entire nations into the kingdom of God, but that when this age ends there will be few still holding to true faith, love, and holiness.[47]

Second: it shows an inclination to place upon God the responsibility to do what he has commanded *us* to do. That is, not to sit around waiting for some mythical revival, but to get out into all the world, preach the gospel, plant many churches, and make ourselves the true salt of the earth.

> ### Don't disguise ineptitude by setting absurd goals

Third: it reflects the old salesman's ploy of disguising ineptitude by setting such a lofty goal that no one can blame him for not achieving it. Did he not aim high? At least he deserves credit for daring great

---

[46]   1 John 5:19; John 12:31; 14:30; 16:11; Matthew 4:8
[47]   Matthew 24:12-13; Luke 18:8; etc.

things! Surely that is praiseworthy, even if his accomplishments were scant?

In the same way, Christians may hide their lack of genuine obedience behind the facade of an artificially excited expectation of imminent revival. "Hey! if it doesn't come, it's God's fault, not ours! Didn't we sing it, speak it, preach it, and pray it? Don't blame us because it never happened!"

Then there is the delusion of confusing the dream with the fact. Singing songs, praying prayers, dreaming dreams about a great outpouring of the Holy Spirit satisfies some Christians as much as if they had experienced the real thing.

Those attitudes do not reflect a genuine God-wrought trust, based upon a God-given promise. They are more likely an excuse to avoid the more difficult, tedious, and unglamorous task of *(a)* praying for one family at a time (instead of an entire city); and *(b)* planting more local churches (instead of waiting for some mythical dream to come true).

Let us just get on with the job, winning one soul at a time, planting one church at a time, nurturing and discipline the people God has placed in our care, working where we are, with what we have - and let the Lord of the harvest decide what the harvest will finally be, and if there will be a vaster outpouring of the Holy Spirit upon the land.

Chapter Five:

ON BUILDING BIGGER BARNS

Preachers who are adept at applying scripture to others sometimes neglect their own instructions. They boldly thrust into others the sword of the Spirit (the word of God), but do not allow its sharp blade to penetrate their own conscience.

Take, for example, Jesus' parable of the *Rich Farmer* (Luke 12:16-21). How often that parable has crossed the pulpit in thunderous rebuke of over-ambitious businessmen! The zealous preacher declaims

> "Your priorities are wrong. Why do you need to make your business so much bigger? Do you really need more wealth? It is sinful to be so busy `building a bigger barn' that you have no time for God, family, or church. Slow down! Change your goals! Obey the scripture! God says that if you have enough for health and happiness, you should be content, not toiling day and night to gather ever larger piles of worthless gold!"

But even while he is rebuking his parishioner, the pastor may be guilty of the same fault. He too is ambitious, craving greater success, yearning for a bigger congregation, a higher income. His head is full of eager plans to pull down his present "barn" and build a bigger one to house the great harvest of souls he confidently anticipates. Look at him! He is no more content with what he has than the lay people he tries to correct. Indeed, some of the most discontented, restless, hard-driving, ambitious, success-hungry people in the church are its pastors. Every day they violate a hundred biblical injunctions against focusing on earthly things more than heavenly, and on tangible things more than spiritual.[48]

---

[48] See Matthew 6:33-34. Sometimes pastors are driven to build an ever bigger church, not because they trust the Lord, but because of some deep insecurity. Jesus spoke about two mind sets; the secular and the spiritual. It is sad to see Christian leaders displaying more of the first than of the second. See also Colossians 3:1-2

Jesus called the rich farmer a "fool". Why should I suppose that his opinion of a pastor who has the same kind of hoarding mind-set is any different?

Isaiah expressed similar anger at "those who add house to house, and join field to field, until everyone else is displaced, and they are left as sole inhabitants of the countryside" (5:8). It was more socially just, more pleasing to God, to have many small landowners than one big one. But does that principle apply only to farmers, or does it speak also to business corporations - and to churches? Which do you suppose serves the interests of the kingdom of God better: one large church; or several smaller ones? Which scenario more equitably disburses the rewards of the kingdom among the people? Which one provides a greater level of satisfaction and fulfillment to the greater number of workers? Which is more likely to bring the greater glory to God?

Those questions are not easy to answer. I cannot, nor do I wish to, deny that God *does* gain high honor from the great churches that are scattered around the world. They have an important place in the divine economy. The same could be said of huge business corporations, vast cattle and sheep stations, and the like. Yet, as we have already discussed, moral philosophers and ethical thinkers across the centuries have unanimously extolled the virtues of the small and spoken disparagingly of the huge. Scripture contains the same teaching. Seldom in Bible days did God favor the grand above the insignificant.[49]

Why do the outwardly successful so often have decayed souls? Because no one can handle greatness without corruption unless his enlargement comes from God. Those who by their own will reach for greatness, reach ultimately for destruction.[50] The only safe path is to ask for no more than God has called each one to attain.

---

[49] 1 Corinthians 1:26-31

[50] Inside the church as well as outside it, these dicta remain true, "Power is apt to corrupt the minds of those who possess it" (William Pitt, from a speech to the House of Lords in 1770). "Power, like a desolating pestilence, pollutes whate'er it touches" (Percy Bysshe Shelly, from his poem "Queen Mab", 1813). "Power tends to corrupt and absolute power corrupts absolutely" (Lord Acton, in a letter to bishop Creighton, 1887).

Has God changed his mind about Babel?	

Remember the *Tower of Babel* and the people who were crushed and scattered by the Lord. What was their fault?[51] They rejected the command of God, who had told them, *"Be fruitful, increase your numbers, and spread out across the earth; people the world and rule over it,"* [52]But they chose instead to *"build a city, and a tower, to make a name for themselves, and to prevent their dispersal over the face of the earth."* They nearly succeeded in their goal. Their temple stood magnificent, majestic, towering over the plain of Shinar, climbing ever higher. God looked at it, and remained unimpressed by their stunning achievement. He wanted *his* will to be done, not *theirs.* Mere size meant nothing to him. How could it, when he is Ruler of the universe? So he crumbled their splendid building back into the dust, and scattered them across the face of the earth. Thus he showed for ever his scorn of the big successes, the lofty structures, the breathtaking monuments, which are so admired by us.

Babel also illustrates God's preferred principle of scattering, rather than gathering everything together in one place. That was a lesson the early church had to learn the hard way - see Acts 8:1.

Is it always wrong to build a bigger barn?	

Does this mean it is sinful to replace a small auditorium with a larger one? Should every big congregation be fragmented? Does God forbid a church to grow bigger and bigger? Is a larger barn always wrong? Of course not. But we *do* need to question our motives, we *do* need to keep testing the assumption that bigger is necessarily better.

Are you a restless pastor, ambitious, yearning for a huge congregation? Let me ask you: *"Why* do you want a larger church?" Can you answer that question in a way that truly agrees with scripture, or will please God? Why *do* you want more and more people? The Lord has already given you a flock. Will a bigger church make you a better or worse shepherd of those sheep? What is driving you along? Are you sure it is

---

[51] Genesis 11:1-9
[52] Genesis 9:1,7.

a godly *vision*? Or is it little more than sordid *ambition*? Are your goals related to the *real* work of the church? If you hunger for a big crowd just to gain a more influential voice in the community, or to be able to change society more effectively, or to be treated with greater honor by civic leaders, and the like, then you are surely moved by a wrong spirit.

Why not build a barn for someone else?

Perhaps there is a better way for a pastor to glorify God. Instead of building a huge new "barn" for himself, he could help provide a home for another congregation. Instead of gathering more and more people into his own fold, he could divide his flock and create another one. And then encourage that one to do the same. Growth by multiplication is usually better than growth by addition!

We all need to learn how to be content with *who* we are, *where* we are, and with *what* God has given us. Thus a wise pastor will simply devote himself to the task of bringing his present flock into true maturity under the lordship of Christ. Which do you think is more important to the Lord: how statistically *successful* a pastor is; or how *faithful*? The pagan monarch Marcus Aurelius understood this principle better than some Christians do -

> "Does the bubble of reputation distract you? [53] Keep before your eyes the swift onset of oblivion, and the abysses of eternity before us and behind; mark how hollow are the echoes of applause, how fickle and undiscerning the judgments of professed admirers, and how puny the arena of human fame. For the entire earth is but a point, and the place of our own habitation but a minute corner in it; and how many are therein who will praise you, and what sort of men are they."

Someone might protest: such self-deprecation was easy for Marcus; he was a king already, he had nowhere to go but down! Yes, but he also recognised that he held his office only by divine providence, and he thought himself no better than any other man. He humbly described his true duty -

---

[53] He is speaking of himself, in his diary.

> "'If thou wouldst know contentment, let thy deeds be few,' said the sage. Better still, limit them strictly to such as are essential, and to such as in a social being reason demands. ... This brings the contentment that comes from doing a few things, and doing them well.
>
> "Test for yourself your capacity for the good man's life; the life of one content with his allotted part in the universe, who seeks only to be just in his doings and charitable in his ways."[54]

Surely then, instead of aping the attitudes and goals of the secular world, the true pastor should focus on the ministry of the word and prayer (Acts 6:4). He can then happily allow the church to grow as large, or stay as small, as the Lord pleases. There is something intrinsically wrong with the man whose main concern is the size of his barn, or whose avowed goal is to build an ever bigger one.

Learn this: God has a wonderful dream for you and me that we can fulfil where we are now, and with what we have already!

Success is not a method, but a man

I have observed a strange phenomenon. If a great church arises in the land, at once pastors of smaller churches flock to it, eager to learn the secrets of its astonishing growth. "Just let me capture the methods used in this place," they say to themselves, "and I will surely achieve the same success in my own city."

But think for a moment. Look at the situation with *"a cool eye"*. The "church growth movement" swept across the nation some twenty-five years ago, and it continues unabated today. Thousands of conferences have come and gone. Tens of thousands of delegates have spent millions of dollars gadding around the planet, gaping at huge churches, mastering new techniques of guaranteed growth. They have purchased mountains of various "how to" manuals. "Church growth" has been on everyone's lips.

---

[54] Op. cit. Bok 4, #4,24,25

But after all that effort and cost, only one thing has measurably changed. Not the size of the average church - which remains much as it has always been, about 100 people - but the frustration quotient of the ministry. Countless pastors who embraced the "bigger is better" syndrome have reaped only a worsening depression and growing hurt.

The scenario is gloomily predictable. With enthusiasm and zeal the delegates come home from their conference, eager to share with their congregations the new things they have learned. But after every new method has fallen exhausted, after vainly trying every new technique - what then? When the fuss and fury have subsided, they and their churches have nothing left except one more notch of disappointment, one further twist of bewilderment.

What the eager conferees forget is that there is no successful *method*, there are only successful *men*, and those men are as diverse as the methods they use. Methods cannot be divorced from the man or woman who employs them, nor from the environment (social, political, cultural, spiritual) in which they proved successful. If my temperament, skills, personality, style are akin to those of the great leader, and if my environment is similar, then his or her method may work for me; yet even then, probably not. Successful leaders do not copy each other; they simply do what is natural and proper for each of them to do, employing techniques, methods, and skills that differ dramatically.

There is no focus on church growth in scripture

I have observed another folly: here is a pastor who promotes growth, yet destroys himself. How does he do it? First, he crosses the ocean to visit a megachurch. Then he returns to his people, glowing with excitement, full of enthusiasm, eager to emulate what he has seen. He tells them to admire the huge church. He praises its enormous size. He commends its many virtues. He sets it before them as an example of true success, and pronounces it an ideal church.

But what is he *really* saying?

Surely something like this: "Our little church hardly deserves the name; it is so small, so insignificant! We have failed God and the surrounding community. I am dissatisfied and disappointed. This church in its present size is hardly worth belonging to!" Why then should he complain if his people take him at his word, and go off and join a bigger congregation? He himself has just told them that bigger is better! He can hardly blame them if they agree with him!

What he should do, of course, is not sing the praises of another man's church, but of his own. Every word he speaks, his ardor, his joy, his whole demeanor, should convey to his people a message that they already belong to the most wonderful church in the world. He would rather be where he is than anywhere else on earth. No one has a better presence of God! No one experiences better answers to prayer! No one enjoys a better worship experience! Any change they make from his church to another could only be a change for the worse!

Have you noticed that there is no focus on church growth in the New Testament? You will search its pages in vain for any instruction on how to build a bigger church. You will find no advice about method or technique. Why? Because scripture assumes that the church must be, and can only be, grown by God.[55] The church is an *organism* more than it is an *organization*; it is the *body* of Christ on earth; therefore God alone can give it life, and grow it, and he alone can determine its shape and size. By contrast, we cannot so much as make one hair grow by one millimetre beyond its divine appointment.[56] Men may build great organizations; but even their most successful creations remain lifeless. Only God can grow a *living thing*.

The pastor's job is like that of a gardener: to fertilize the soil, to plant the seed, to water the plant, to dig up the weeds, and to drive off the pests. Then God (*who alone is able*) will bring each plant to its full flowering beauty. So the biblical focus is upon *character*, not *achievement*. If a pastor gives attention to building a godly character, and to faithful teaching and ministry, God himself will grow the church he wants in that place, and the size of it can be left in God's hands. A properly functioning congregation will increase in whatever way God has appointed for it.[57]

---

[55] 1 Corinthians 3:5-7

[56] Matthew 5:36

[57] See 1 Timothy 4:11-16. Three times Paul couples two ideas together; let Timothy simply give attention to himself, and to sound doctrine, and he will then save both himself and his hearers. You might (continued on next page)

Our focus is so often wrong. We somehow persuade ourselves that the future of the church absolutely depends upon our strenuous labors. We forget that any time the Father wants to increase the number of Christian worshippers, he can do so with a flick of his finger. All he needs is a pile of pebbles![58] That God refrains from doing so (despite countless prayer meetings over the years, and much fervent pleading for "a great harvest of souls") shows that we are reaching for the wrong thing. God apparently has priorities that are higher than the size of our churches!

> ## No living thing can grow beyond God's appointed limit

A gardener may plant many flowers; but he cannot make one of them grow bigger than the laws of God allow. The only way he can force a flower to be more than the Lord intended, is to make an artificial one. Then he can shape it any way he likes, and make it as big as he pleases. But who would prefer blossoms of silk, or plastic, or even gold, silver, or jewels, to replace every living flower in the garden?

Similarly, clever people can build an artificial church, changing it from an organism to an organization, and make it as big as ambition and skill allow. Like a platinum orchid, it may look beautiful, and possess value, but is it a *church*? Size and external loveliness alone will not answer that question. You will need to look for evidence that it was built by God, that it is truly *alive*, that it displays the proper attributes of the body of Christ. The *Letters to the Seven Churches* in the *Apocalypse*[59] show that not every corporate body that appears to be a church on earth is recognised as such in heaven!

So what should a pastor do when someone urges him to attend still another church growth conference? My advice is: stay home! There are better things he can do with your money. Why does he need to learn how to build a church God has not called him to build, using methods

---

(continued from previous page) find it advantageous to reflect on that. It is the shortest and simplest manual on church growth you will ever read. Paul seemed to think it was adequate enough!

[58] Matthew 3:9; Luke 3:9.

[59] Revelation 2:1, ff.

God has not equipped him to use? He may do better, and get more value for his dollar, by taking his wife out to a romantic dinner![60]

Can you count the days that are yet to come?

Laziness and cowardice have no place in the kingdom of God. Scripture everywhere demands that we labor industriously in the service of God, and do so with an expectation of good success. Yet the same scriptures warn with equal passion against presumption. No one knows what tomorrow will bring, whether good or ill. Which means that we must be willing to accept the providence of God in all things -

> *"When the time of year is right for each new crop, get up early and sow your seed. Do not slacken off from your toil until the evening, because you do not know which sowing will flourish. Perhaps this harvest will be successful, or that one; or perhaps they will both be bountiful"[61]*

> *"I understand, Lord, that no one can choose his own place in life; I know that no one can predict or control the outcome of his labor"[62]*

The unknown author of the apocryphal 2 Esdras confronted this dilemma. He told a story about Ezra lying on his bed in Babylon, deeply perplexed because Zion lay in desolation while haughty Babylon grew ever richer and mightier. Ezra pleaded with God to explain the seeming injustice of his providence -

> "I had thought that perhaps those in Babylon lead better lives, and that is why Zion is in subjection. But when I arrived here, I saw wickedness beyond reckoning. ... My

---

[60] There are, of course, valid reasons for visiting successful churches; to rejoice in what God has wrought; enriching fellowship; the enlargement that travel brings; a well earned vacation; and the like. I am speaking only against the position that success must be measured primarily by statistical achievement, and depends upon discovering and using certain techniques of growth. You should not allow yourself to be imprisoned by demands to do what God has not equipped you to do.

[61] Ecclesiastes 11:6.

[62] Jeremiah 10:23

heart sank because I observed how you tolerate sinners and spare the godless, how you have destroyed your own people but preserved your enemies. You have given no indication to anyone how your ways are to be understood!"[63]

The story-teller continues Ezra's complaint across many paragraphs, climaxing with the lament -

"My heart is tortured every hour as I strive to understand the ways of the Most High, and to fathom even part of his judgment." (5:34)

Suddenly, an angel stood before Ezra, and told him that he never would in this life probe the mysteries of God's providence. Ezra demanded, "Why not, my lord?" He got the same answer Job was given - a nature lesson!

"Count me the days that are not yet come, collect the scattered rain drops for me, make the withered flowers bloom again, unlock for me the storehouses and let loose the winds shut up there, or give visible form to a voice - then I shall answer your question about the trials of Israel."(5:36,37)

Ezra had no choice but to admit his helplessness to meet the angelic challenge, so he had to be content to accept by faith that God's love is truly unfailing, his ultimate purpose inscrutable, his sovereignty incontestable (vs. 38-40). The Lord God is not obliged either to explain or to justify his actions to any creature. We must therefore echo the words of Paul, who allowed that even he saw the purpose of God as though he were looking through a smoky glass;[64] none of us can be sure of the shape the events of each new day will take.

James, too, warns us sternly against presumption -

"Listen to me you who keep on saying, `Today or tomorrow we will travel to this town, or to that one, and stay there a year, buying and selling and making

---

[63]   2 Esdras 3:1-3, 28-31, 43 Revised English Bible

[64]   1 Corinthians 13:12

money.' Yet none of you has the slightest notion of what might happen tomorrow. Don't you know what your life is? Nothing more than a mist, which appears for a little while, and then vanishes again. What you should be saying is this: 'Unless the Lord approves, we cannot even stay alive, let alone do this or that!'" (4:13-16).

Perhaps the Lord will let us build the castle of our dreams. Perhaps he will not. Better, simply find God's dream, and for so long as he gives us days and health, devote ourselves to fulfilling it.

Chapter Six:

LEARN TO SAY "NO!"

The apostles never show in any of their letters the slightest interest in the numerical size or growth of the churches they addressed. Consider, for example, Paul's letters to his young disciples, Timothy and Titus. Where is there even a breath of a suggestion about technique or method for building a bigger church? Paul shows no concern about the number of bodies occupying the pews in the churches his friends pastored. No doubt he *was* interested in the growth of those churches - after all, the gospel *is* about gathering multitudes of men and women into the kingdom of God. But Paul knew that the harvest was God's responsibility, not his. So the size of a particular congregation was low on his list of priorities.

Instead, everywhere from Romans to Jude, the focus remains the same: not statistics, but *character.*

Consider these scriptures, and many others like them -

1 Corinthians 1:20-21. There is a humbling declaration! The preacher's task, says Paul, is not a work of wisdom, but of folly! We do not stand among the clever, but among buffoons! That is because God has determined that the world will never discover him through its smart knowledge, but only by humble acceptance of his grace. Unhappily, we preachers have no more liking for that decree than does the world. We prefer to present ourselves as wise, noble, important, and we crave admiration and the plaudits of a clamoring throng. We often yearn to be as much loved by the world as by the church.

We would do better to copy Paul, and to reckon ourselves the earth's dung.[65] Much pompous strutting would then be abandoned, and we would be content to be the slaves of all, and not their masters. We might even grow to be more like Christ.[66]

---

[65] 1 Corinthians 4:13.
[66] John 13:12-17.

Ecclesiastes 4:13-16. We should apply Solomon's sobering reflections to our own position, ministry, or work. Even if *"there is no end to the host of people you lead"*, eventually you will be as forgotten as the man who pastored the tiniest flock. Better to remain a humble shepherd who can heed advice, than to become a powerful ruler, too big to listen to lesser people. Before the throne of God, nothing will count but character. Our mightiest works are less than a grain of dust to the Ruler of Galaxies.

1 Timothy 6:3-10. This passage I want to paraphrase, replacing the thought of "money" with that of "success", for the two can be taken as synonymous -

> *"Do you want true success and prosperity? Then search for them in godliness and contentment. We brought nothing into this world, and we can't take anything out of it. People who yearn for success open themselves to many temptations. They become trapped by foolish and ruinous ambitions, which have plunged countless men and women into chaos and destruction. The love of success is the root of many evils. Some people, hungry for success, have wandered away from the faith and brought upon themselves untold miseries and regrets. But you, man of God, flee from all this craving for success, and pursue instead righteousness, godliness, integrity, love, resilience, and gentleness."*

Need I say more - except perhaps to suggest that you read the passage again? Replace "people" with "pastor", and the idea of "success" with that of a "big church". Then ask yourself again: how does a pastor who craves a large, flourishing congregation, and a handsome salary, differ in his ambition from the businessman who hungers for commercial success and wealth?

Mark again Paul's closing injunction to Timothy -

> *"If you are a man of God, **these are the things you should pursue:** righteousness, godliness, integrity, love, resilience, and gentleness."*[67]

---

[67] Verse 11.

Which raises this question: how much time and energy - in relation to the frantic hours most pastors spend on programs, projects, performance and profit - do you devote to those biblical concerns? Do you perhaps apply Paul's dictates to your people, but forget to apply them to yourself?

Cobblestones are enough for God

Let me repeat: the biblical rule is, who we *are* is far more important in the eyes of God than what we *do*. He values character above accomplishment. How could it be otherwise? A thousand things over which we have no control determine what we will do in life. Did we have any say in where we were born and when? Did we decide what personality and skills we brought into the world, what spiritual gifts and office in the church God gave us, what social environment we have to contend with? Can we fix what opportunity we will find or opposition we will face, what spiritual climate surrounds us, or the like?

Consider the martyrs: what chance did they have for great achievement in the world? Yet are they any less honored by God because their lives and ministry were cut short? Less dramatically, what will you say to a gifted preacher who is immobilized by an accident, and must spend the rest of his life a helpless, speechless, cripple? Has he been robbed of his reward? Or will God judge him on the nobility of his character, and on how well his behavior reflects the beauty of Christ, rather than on a ministry success rendered impossible by life's vicissitudes?

This is surely at least part of the meaning of Matthew 3:9, that God needs neither you nor me for anything. Whatever he wants to do lies entirely in his own hand, even to raising up worshippers from the cobblestones in the street. That he refrains from doing so shows he is far less anxious about the size of a congregation than we are. If it really worried the Almighty that a church is so small, he could soon enough add thousands to it! We could all profit by meditating more deeply on Matthew 6:25-34, and then listen to what it says about our goals in life.

John Knox, the Scottish Reformer, renowned for his furious battle-cry, *The First Blast of the Trumpet Against the Monstrous Regimen of Women*,[68] was captured by the French in 1547 and condemned to serve as

---

[68] The title of a pamphlet he published in 1558. The "woman" was the unhappy queen, Mary Tudor. Unfortunately for Knox, (continued on next page)

a galley slave. He toiled at the oars and under the lash for nearly two years before his friends were able to secure his release. Suppose however that he had not escaped, or had died while chained to the oars, as many did? He would have perished in obscurity, his work done by another. But would that have lessened his standing in the kingdom of God? Not unless he had allowed his bondage to embitter his soul.

John Wesley was once captured by a British press gang and forcibly carried onto a war ship. He escaped by seizing an opportunity one night to leap overboard and swim ashore. Suppose he had been unable to swim (which few could do in those days), or the opportunity to escape had not presented itself, or he had died at sea in a battle? He too would have been soon forgotten and another raised up by God to do his work. Yet would that have lessened his success as a man and a Christian?

What I have said about Knox and Wesley *was* of course the fate of many fine people. Some were burned at the stake; others were unable to shake off their fetters and endured life-long imprisonment; others labored wretchedly as slaves until death gave them sweet release. Thomas Fuller tells the story of a brave Englishman who had *both* experiences, first of long misery, and then of escape, yet through it all he kept his faith -

Job Hartop - Soldier & Slave

"*Job Hartop* (sailed in 1568) with Sir John Hawkins, his general, to make discoveries in New Spain. (He was) chief gunner in her majesty's ship called the *Jesus of Lubeck...* Long and dangerous was his journey, eight of his men at Cape Verde being killed, and the general himself wounded with poisoned arrows, but was cured by a negro drawing out the poison with a clove of garlic, enough to make nice noses dispense with the valiant smell for the sanative virtue thereof... *Job* was his name and patience was with him, so that he may pass amongst the confessors[69] of this country. For, being with some

---

(continued from previous page) Elizabeth ascended the throne shortly after his pamphlet was published, and it made his name odious in the English court. He is also linked with the saying engraved on his monument in Geneva: "A man with God is always in the majority".

[69] That is, a true Christian.

other by this general, for want of provisions, left on land, after many miseries they came to Mexico, and he continued a prisoner twenty-three years, viz. two years in Mexico, one year in the Contractation-house[70] in Seville, another in the Inquisition-house in Triana, twelve years in the galleys, four years (with the cross of St Andrew on his back) in the Everlasting Prison, and three years a drudge to Hernando de Soria, to so high a sum did the inventory of his sufferings amount.

"So much of his patience, now see the end[71] which the Lord made with him. Whilst enslaved to the aforesaid Hernando, he was sent to sea in a Flemish ship, which was afterward taken by an English ship, called the Galleon Dudley, *and so was he safely landed at Portsmouth, December 2, 1590.*"[72]

Cast your eye again over that "inventory of his sufferings", and imagine what your reactions or attitudes would have been to 23 years of such wretched bondage. Would your faith still be strong and your patience unshaken? After two years of torment in the hands of the Inquisition, twelve years of merciless toil at the oars, four years strapped to a heavy weight, and three years the slave of a despotic lord, would your loyalty to Christ stand firm? How long he had to wait before his prayers were finally answered! Who can measure the boundaries of such tenacious courage?

He built no great church, he won no host of souls; chains and drudgery consumed the best years of his life; yet surely he stands among the great in the kingdom of God, a "worthy confessor" of Christ. His work was the best

---

[70] A place from which slaves were contracted out to work as laborers.

[71] Echoing James 5:11, KVJ.

[72] From Fuller's Worthies: edited from the original by Richard Barber; The Folio society, London 1987; pg 237, 238. The original, "The Worthies of England'" was first published in 1662, and has been often reprinted. Thomas Fuller was an Anglican divine and historian, reputed to have been perhaps the first writer ever to make a full-time living from his pen.

anyone can do: continuing to yield the fragrance of Christ despite the most awful trials.[73]

God values the worker more than the work

Am I saying that the things you and I accomplish for God have no significance, that we need only worry about being good, and not doing good? Of course not. What we do in life and how we do it inescapably reflects what we are. Our works inexorably reveal the measure of our obedience to the Father's will - whether we have done too much or too little.

Yet always God remains more concerned about the worker than the work. If any of us fail as Christians, then stupendous success in ministry, far from doing us good, may well increase the wrath of God against us. But if we succeed as men or women of God, constantly growing the sweet fruit of the Spirit, then we may happily leave our worldly success in the hands of God.

The Roman philosopher, dramatist, and politician Seneca was sent into exile by his former pupil and friend, the emperor Nero (who later compelled him to suicide). During the time of his banishment, Seneca wrote a number of treatises, in one of which he commented on the manner in which he found consolation for his fate -

> "For how little, we should ask ourselves, have we lost, when we may take with us into (exile) our two most desirable possessions: our contact with universal nature; and our own character? It was, I am sure, the very intention of the Creator of the world... that none but a man's most worthless possessions should pass into the control of another man. All that is most valuable to a man lies beyond the reach of other men's power. Such possessions can neither be given nor taken away. The universe around us, that most grand and elaborate work of nature, and the mind that can contemplate and marvel at it... are our own everlasting property. ... Let us

---

[73] You can gain a better sense of the enormity of Mr. Hartop's sufferings – especially his twelve years at the oar of a galley – from the description you will find in the addendum at the end of this chapter.

therefore go on our way, wherever it may lead us, fearlessly, with eager and uplifted heart. Let us fare to whatever land we must; no place on the face of the earth can (really be for us) a place of exile... "[74]

The Lebanese poet-philosopher Kahlil Gibran (1883-1931), expressed the same idea in quite different terms: how the soul, when it soars to meet its God must leave behind all the trammeling weights of this world-

> "Fain would I take with me all that is here. But how can I? A voice cannot carry the tongue and the lips that give it wings. Alone must it seek the ether. And alone and without his nest shall the eagle fly across the sun."[75]

We can carry nothing better into the Father's presence than a life that in every way has reflected the beauty of Christ.

Serve God, not some elusive goal of "success"

The prerogative must remain God's: to give us whatever increase pleases him; or, like Fuller's worthy gunner, to allow life to deny us any hope of outward prosperity. Our task is to serve him, *not some elusive and possibly unattainable goal of statistical "success"*.

Have you ever realized that in the eyes of this world, the scandal of Jesus is not what he did, but what he did not do. They ask: why did he not protest against the tyranny of Rome, or against the horrors of slavery, and the hideous gladiatorial contests. Why did he remain silent about the arenas, where living people were torn and eaten by wild beasts for the amusement of the populace?

He knew that every large town had its child brothels, where little boys and girls were sold for the pleasure of soul-weary men who had lost all pity and scruple. When they were about eight years of age, and their bones no longer supple, the children were cast into the gutter to die. Yet Jesus raised no cry for their rescue.

---

[74] Seneca: Four Tragedies and Octavia; tr. By E.F. Watling; Penguin Classics, 1970; pg. 314. The passage quoted comes from Seneca's "Ad Halviam Matrem" (VIII).

[75] The Prophet; Alfred A. Knopf, New York, 1968; pg. 4.

Throughout the dominions of Rome travelers could hear the screams of those who were being dismembered in its torture chambers; but Jesus spoke no protest against such barbarity. Nor did he condemn the political collaborators who were betraying his own people. Indeed, he ignored most of the terrible social evils of his time, and concentrated primarily on matters of religion and personal morality.

Measure that silence of Jesus against the numerous protest movements of our time. Compare him with the worthy people who are striving passionately to rid our world of its prejudice, conflict, violence, and inequality. Then you will understand why many good people in this world find offence in Christ.

> **There has never been a less driven man than Jesus**

Perhaps you too have wondered why Jesus, confronted with so many moral enormities, addressed hardly any of them. The reason is simple: *there has never been a less driven man than Jesus of Nazareth.* No one set his agenda for him; no one wrote his calendar; no one drew up his time-table or told him what he had to do. The merely urgent never compelled Christ, nor the important, nor even the necessary. One thing alone governed his daily choices: *his perception of the Father's will.*[76] Christ did nothing, he spoke nothing, outside of what the Father had commanded. So his daily life was marked by a serenity, a control, a calmness, that is truly astonishing.

How far removed his example is from our tendency to anxious, compulsive, driven behavior! How easily the thousand pressing clamors of each new day draw us away from the purpose of God! Yet watch Jesus as he calmly ignores two blind beggars, walks past them, goes into a house, and closes the door in their face!

Can you imagine yourself possessing such certainty about the work given you by God, or about your freedom to snub compassionate demands? Most people would be battered by guilt every step along the road if they rebuffed a blind man who called for help - and a thousand times more if he were calling them by *name*! They would simply have to turn back, speak to him, and at the very least offer him some money! Yet *Jesus*

---

[76] See John 8:28, 38, 12:50; 14:10; 5:36; 9:4; 10:25; etc.

gave those men neither words nor shekels nor even a look. He shunned their persistent cries, even when they were stumbling along the road behind him. He simply walked on, and into the house, as if they were not there.[77]

Then watch Jesus ignoring the scores of sick, infirm, crippled people at Bethesda, while healing only one man. Could you have been so sure of yourself? Wouldn't you have felt obliged to preach a sermon, offer a prayer, or at least move around among the sufferers, murmuring some word of comfort or hope? And after the cripple was healed, think of the opportunity Jesus missed for a great revival meeting! The air was crackling with excitement and expectancy. Everybody was looking for him. What a moment to preach repentance and faith! What a harvest of souls he could have reaped! It is difficult to imagine any modern healing evangelist working such a miracle on one cripple and then walking away from scores of others without so much as a word! But Jesus was not driven like we are. He did not allow the compulsions that so often dominate our behavior to push him around.[78]

He was willing to let them perish

Look at the stunning assertion in Mark 6:48. Jesus was apparently willing to walk past that flotilla, and leave all on board the ships to perish in the stormy sea! Do you balk at that? Then remember that he is still doing the same today. He constantly passes by people who are about to die on the freeway, or in the air, or on the sea. He offers them no help unless they compel his attention by bold prayer and vigorous faith. Even then his intervention is not always found. Despite their most fervent pleas, many a faithful child of God has perished miserably, torn apart by

---

[77] Matthew 9:27 ff; 20:29 ff. The sense of the Greek text in both places is that Jesus had walked up to where they were sitting, and had gone past them without pausing. The idea is that he firmly intended to go on, and did not wish to be delayed. If they had not pressed him to help them, he would have been content to leave them sitting in darkness on the dusty roadside. Someone might protest that Jesus did not really ignore the blind men, that he was actually trying to provoke them to faith, that he wanted them to follow him. That may be so, although Matthew gives no suggestion of it. In any case, the fact remains: if they had not found the courage and tenacity to pursue him, he would still have left them blind and begging.

[78] John 5:1-9.

pain. They received perhaps inner fortitude from God, but not the miracle for which they had yearned.

Could you do such things? Could you remain silent and unmoved in the presence of a crowd of sick people who were waiting for a miracle from God? Could you hear a blind man calling your name in the street, yet refrain from restoring his sight, or at least giving him some alms? Could you see people drowning in a river and walk on unheeding?

Jesus apparently could do all those things, while remaining untroubled in his mind and spirit. Nothing and no one compelled him, except the voice of the Father.

That is a grace we should cultivate. Instead, we tend to be a compulsive people, wrought upon by ambition (rather than true vision), commanded by the expectations of other people, controlled by secular demands, pressured by our peers, deafened by the hubbub of a thousand cries for help! It is a miracle if we catch even a line or two of the Father's plan!

We should not do things because they are noble, necessary, nice, or even good, grave, or glorious, but only because they are what the Father has given us to do. If all God's servants were busy doing only what he has commanded for each of them, how splendid the church would be.

Ah! that every Christian might be shamed by the prayer of one of another faith, Ibrahim ibn Adham, an early Muslim saint. He was born a prince of Balkh, but he heard a voice calling him to renounce his splendid palace, and to serve God alone. So he obeyed, and became a hermit, with a cave his only dwelling. His habitual plea was only this -

> "Oh God, raise me out of the shame of disobedience to
> the glory of submission to thee!"[79]

Those who shoulder the yoke of Christ, will find it sits easy. Those who pick up the burden of the Lord, will find its weight light. Upon them abundant grace will fall. They have waited on God, refusing to be driven by the demands of others. So they soar on eagle's wings; they run, but

---

[79] The Ruba'iyat of Omar Khayyam; tr. By Peter Avery & John Heath-Stubbs; Penguin Books, London, 1983; pg. 96. The prince-hermit died in the year 777

never fall exhausted; they march, and their strength is constantly renewed.[80]

Now comes an obvious question: how do I know what God wants from me? How can I come to the serenity of saying "yes" to each instruction that comes from the Father, but "no" to every other demand, regardless of how urgent or important it may seem?

Much of the answer to those questions can be found in Paul's remaining instructions to Timothy, beginning with the one that opens the next part of this book.

---

[80]   Isaiah 40:29-31; and cp. Colossians 1:29;etc.

ADDENDUM

In his dramatic novel The Sea-Hawk, Rafael Sabatini (whose writings were noted for their meticulous attention to historical accuracy) describes the living hell endured by a galley slave in the 16th century. Many a Protestant English seaman, captured by the Spaniards and enslaved as heretics, suffered miseries similar to those of Sir Oliver Tressilian (the hero of the story) -

> "The galley to which our gentleman was dispatched was a vessel of fifty oars, each manned by seven men. They were seated upon a sort of staircase that followed the slope of the oar, running from the gangway in the vessel's middle down to the shallow bulwarks.

> "The place allotted to Sir Oliver was that next the gangway. Here, stark naked as when he was born, he was chained to the bench, and in those chains let us say at once he remained without a single moment's intermission for six months.[81]

> "Between himself and the hard timbers of his seat there was naught but flimsy and dirty sheepskin. From end to end the bench was not more than ten feet in length, whilst the distance separating it from the next one was a bare four feet. In that cramped space of ten feet by four Sir Oliver and his six oar-mates had their miserable existence, waking and sleeping - for they slept in their chains at the oars without sufficient room in which to lie at stretch.

> "Anon Sir Oliver became hardened and inured to that unspeakable existence, that living death of the galley-slave. ... For spells of six or eight endless hours at a time, and on one occasion for no less than ten hours, did he pull at his oar without a single moment's pause. With one foot on the stretcher, the other on the bench in front

---

[81] And would have remained there until he died, except that the ship was taken by Muslims, much as happened to Job Hartop in real life.

of him, grasping his part of that appallingly heavy fifteen-foot oar, he would bend his back to thrust forward - and upwards so as to clear the shoulders of the groaning, sweating slaves in front of him - then he would lift the end so as to bring the blade down to the water, and having gripped he would rise from his seat to throw his full weight into the pull, and so fall back with clank of chain upon the groaning bench to swing forward once more, and so on until his senses reeled, his sight became blurred, his mouth parched, and his whole body a living, straining ache. Then would come the sharp fierce cut of the boatswain's whip to revive energies that flagged however little, and sometimes to leave a bleeding stripe upon his naked back.

"Thus day in and day out, now broiled and blistered by the pitiless southern sun, now chilled by the night dews whilst he took his cramped and unrefreshing rest, indescribably filthy and disheveled, his hair and beard matted with endless sweat, unwashed save by the rains which in that season were all too rare, choked almost by the stench of his miserable comrades and infested by filthy crawling things begotten of decaying sheepskins and Heaven alone knows what other foulnesses of that floating hell. He was sparingly fed upon weevilled biscuit and vile messes of tallowy rice, and to drink he was given luke-warm water that was often stale, saving that sometimes when the spell of rowing was more than usually protracted the boatswain would thrust lumps of bread sodden in wine into the mouths of the toiling slaves to sustain them."[82]

Slaves who became ill were simply thrown overboard; those who collapsed or refused to work were flogged until they complied or died. To endure such a life (as Job Hartop did) for twelve years was an act of astonishing courage and personal discipline. To escape from it without hatred or bitterness as some Christian slaves apparently did, was even

---

[82] Cherry Tree Books, London, 1937; Part Two, Chapter Two, "The Renegade," pg. 77-78

more amazing, and a singular testimony to the sustaining grace of God. I wonder if I could have done so well?

Proposition Two:

DUTY –

"Fulfill all the duties God has given you."

Chapter Seven:

PREACH THE WORD

Remember that we are looking at Paul's four instructions to Timothy:[83]

> *always keep a cool head*
> *fulfil every God-given duty*
> *labor to spread the gospel*
> *put up with hardship.*

In this section we take up the second of those instructions -

> *"Fulfil all the duties God has given you."*

What are those duties? Across the centuries a consensus has emerged among theologians that all the vital duties of the pastor(s) of a local church can be reduced to three items:

> *WORD*
> *SACRAMENT*
> *DISCIPLINE*

Any task beyond those three is extraneous to the real work of the ministry. But when those duties are properly fulfilled by the *pastors*, then the congregation will be able to do *its* appointed work. That is, the people will be properly equipped to reach out to the community in *evangelism*. When the shepherds faithfully guard and guide their flock, and when the flock is fruitful in reproducing itself through evangelism, then the church will truly be the Body of Christ in its locality. It will be to its neighbors everything that Jesus himself would be if he were there in the flesh.

The first of those three duties is to *preach the word*, which is the primary task of the ministry. Above this, nothing should be allowed to take pre-eminence. Think about Paul. How difficult it is to over-emphasise the importance he gave to preaching. Turn where you will in his letters, you will find him pressing the need for constant instruction in the truth of the gospel. Consider for example the verses that come just before our text -

---

[83] 2 Timothy 4:5.

"As one who is standing in the presence of God and before Christ Jesus - who will judge both the living and the dead - and in the light of his coming again to establish his kingdom, I earnestly charge you: preach the message of God. Press it upon the people, whether it is convenient or inconvenient. Persuade them, rebuke them, encourage them, never give way to them. Patiently persist in your teaching, because you know that a time is coming when they will no longer want to hear sound doctrine."[84]

There is no higher task, there is no more noble calling, than to proclaim the "unsearchable riches of Christ." That does not mean the task is pleasurable. No one has ever promised that the teacher's mission would bring popularity. People are no more enamored of sound doctrine today than they have ever been. Nonetheless, they need to hear it; and the pastor must preach it, in season and out of season, whether the people like it or not, for the spiritual shepherd has no sublimer duty.

A faithful pastor will present the Word of God to his flock in three ways: explained; revealed; prophetic -

THE EXPLAINED WORD

Nehemiah provides a fine example of what this means. During his life there occurred one of the major turning-points in history. For the first time ever, a pulpit was built, and a man stood on it for the express purpose of reading aloud and teaching the scriptures.[85] That man was Ezra, who was there at the behest of the people: *"they urged Ezra the scribe to bring out the Book of the Law of Moses, which the Lord had given to Israel"* (verse 1).

The scribe's heart was deeply stirred by this extraordinary clamor for the word of God. So he hastily caused a pulpit to be erected, and there he stood for six hours, reading and expounding the law of the Lord. The people, young and old, gave earnest attention to every word. Here is a truism: good preaching requires good listening. The poorest speaker can

---

[84]   2 Timothy 4:1-3a

[85]   Nehemiah 8:1-12. Verse 4 ("Ezra the scribe stood on a wooden pulpit that had been made for this purpose") is the first mention in literature of a pulpit

be lifted to eloquence if he is faced by an enthusiastic and attentive audience.

We preachers need to teach our people how to be devout hearers of the word of God, rather than listeners to clever sermons. It is substantially our own fault that the people have "itching ears", and only want to hear "good" preachers. We have exalted the preacher above the pulpit; the messenger above the message; the worker above the word. The people must learn, not just to hear a sermon, but to listen for the voice of God.

The problem of poorly instructed audiences is not a new one. A thousand years ago, a lady-in-waiting of the imperial Japanese court noticed the same problem in the Buddhist temples of her time -

> "A preacher ought to be good-looking. For, if we are properly to understand his worthy sentiments, we must keep our eyes on him while he speaks; should we look away, we may forget to listen. Accordingly, an ugly preacher may well be the source of sin...
>
> "But I really must stop writing this kind of thing. If I were still young enough, I might risk the consequence of putting down such impieties, but at my present stage of life I should be less flippant.
>
> "Some people, on hearing that a priest is particularly venerable and pious rush off to the temple where he is preaching, determined to arrive before anyone else. They, too, are liable to bring a load of sin on themselves, and would do better to stay away. ...
>
> "Often one hears exchanges like this: 'There was a service at such-and-such a temple, where they did the Eight Lessons.' 'Was Lady So-and-So present?' 'Of course. How could she possibly have missed it?' It really is too bad that they should always answer like this."[86]

---

[86] The Pillow book of Sei Shonagon' tr. Ivan Morris, Penguin Classics, London, 1967; Selection 21; pg. 53. Her comments about the good-looking preacher are, of course, a piece of impudent sarcasm.

Good preaching is better than an angelic visitation

A good pastor instructs his people in their duty to concentrate upon the word. He instills into them a hunger for the bread of life. Then they will become like the congregation Ezra faced, where *"all the people gave their full attention to the Book of the Law."* [87] Their focus was not on the preacher, but on his function as a messenger of God.

Mark this extraordinary passage from Martin Luther -

> "The Word of God is the greatest, most necessary, and most important thing in Christendom. For the Sacraments cannot be without the Word, but the Word may well be without the Sacraments...
>
> "Even if I heard angels preach in their majesty, I would not be more moved by it than I am now by hearing my pastor or another preacher preach. If people were sure that what they hear is the Word of God, they would not snore so and be so lazy and secure. But because they think mere men are speaking, and that it is man's word they hear, they become unreasonable beasts. They sigh and mourn because original sin is so strong even in the regenerated...
>
> Indeed, if the matter were in my hands, I would not want God to speak to me from heaven or to appear to me. But I do want - and this is my daily prayer - that I might duly honor and esteem the brethren who have grace and the Holy Spirit, and who by the preaching of the Word console, strengthen, exhort, admonish, and teach me. What better or more useful appearance of God would you desire?"[88]

---

[87] Verse 3. Notice also the remarkable reverence they showed for the open Bible – verses 5-6.

[88] Paraphrases from a series of sayings in Items #2858, 2873, 2875, in Volume Two of what Luther Says; compiled by Ewald M Plass; Concordia Publishing House, Missouri; 1959. It is not difficult to imagine the snort of disgust with which Luther would greet those who claim the essence of piety is to pray for an outpouring of the Spirit that will sweep away (continued on next page)

Similarly, a passage in the early second century document known as *The Didache* urges the disciple of Christ to revere the preacher -

> "By day and by night, my son, remember him who
> speaks the word of God to you. Give him the honor you
> would give the Lord; for wherever the Lord's attributes
> are the subject of discourse, there the Lord is present."[89]

Preacher, is that your attitude? You can hardly expect people to listen to you with patience, and to seek the supernatural revelation of heaven behind the facade of your sermons, unless you yourself adopt the same attitude toward other preachers. We must learn how to look past the carrier and perceive the truth of God. Whenever the scriptures are open, and a man or woman teaches from them faithfully, there is some word of the Lord to be heard. Even the mightiest among us can gain heavenly instruction from those who are least.

Paul said that the teacher's task requires much patience.[90] Our story in Nehemiah shows this. They began at six in the morning, and did not finish until noon. Across those hours Ezra first read a portion of scripture, and then the Levites explained the passage to the people. When all the Levites had finished, Ezra read another passage, which was then explained, and so on. Both the teachers and the learners displayed unwearied patience. The Levites, we are told, "helped the people to understand the law, while the people remained in their places" - good teachers and good listeners co-operating together to fulfil the purpose of God.

Nehemiah emphasized this mutual endeavor, by twice insisting upon it -

> *"They read from the Book of the Law of God, made its*
> *sense clear, interpreted its meaning, and kept on*

(continued from last page) sermon and make the pulpit unnecessary! They would do better to pray for their preacher to preach better, and for themselves to be better hearers.

[89] "Didache" is an abbreviation of the full name of the document, which is "The Teaching of the Twelve Apostles". It is a manual of instruction about church life and practice. From Early Christian Writings: translated by Maxwell Staniforth; Penguin Books, 1968; "The Didache" I.4 pg 229.

[90] 2 Timothy 4:2

instructing the people until they thoroughly understood the reading."[91]

If we had more such teachers, and more such listeners, we might more often enjoy the result they experienced -

"They celebrated the day with great gladness, because they had understood everything that was declared to them."

On the contrary, in many parts of the church today, congregations are more prone to fulfil Paul's sad prediction -

"A time is coming when people will no longer want to hear sound doctrine, but with itchy ears they will gather around themselves teachers who say only pleasant things; they will turn away from listening to the truth, and prefer to hear fables instead."[92]

But we dare not yield to such pressures. The command is urgent -

"Devote yourself to the public reading of scripture, and to exhortation and teaching... These matters should be your first concern, nothing else should have higher priority; thus everyone will recognise the good progress you are making. Keep a close watch both over yourself and over your teaching, so that you never slacken in either way. Then you will be sure of saving both yourself and your hearers."[93]

Observe Paul's remarkable confidence. To ensure success in his ministry, Timothy needed only to guard his own integrity and to teach sound doctrine! The rest could be left in the hands of God.

To many people, "sound doctrine" sounds ominous

But to many people, "sound doctrine" has an ominous ring. They argue that too much emphasis on doctrine splits congregations apart, builds

---

[91]   Verses 8 and 12.

[92]   2 Timothy 4:3-4

[93]   1 Timothy 4:13, 15-16.

arrogant self-satisfaction, hinders the numerical growth of the church, stifles freedom and life; and the like.

They may sometimes be right. But sound doctrine also unites the people around a common faith; it builds passionate loyalty to the church; it creates deep and lasting commitment.

I know that doctrine has been the cause of some terrible quarrels, even of bloodshed, across the long history of the church. But at least those warring saints had something to quarrel about; at least they had something to die for! But a single drop of blood would be too much to spill for the saccharine gospel that often disgraces today's pulpits.. Who would shed even one tear for this emaciated, castrated message? Pleasant on the ear, untroubling to the soul, it cost the preacher no pain and is unworthy of any by the hearers.

Oh! for a people again who know *what* they believe; who know *why* they believe it; who believe it fervently enough to *die* rather than abandon one sentence of it!

I am not arguing for some kind of blind dogmatism, nor violent prejudice, nor jeering rejection of anyone who disagrees with me. We must all have a life-long willingness to go on learning. Pity those who are unable to cast aside mistaken ideas, or to honor and love others who look through different eyes, or hear with different ears.

> "If a man does not keep pace with his companions, perhaps it is because he hears a different drummer. Let him step to the music which he hears, however measured or far away."[94]

Nonetheless, while we should respect every person's right to form his or her own conviction, our personal beliefs should stand firm. In that commitment to sound doctrine we find both stability and strength, and we bring the same to our hearers. *"You will save both yourself,"* said Paul, *"and those you teach, if you give top priority to sound doctrine!"*

None of this is easy. It is hard labor to learn the word of God properly, and it is hard labor to teach it. Scripture itself acknowledges this in the many places (especially in Proverbs) where it speaks of the toil required

---

[94]   Henry David Thoreau, in "Conclusion" to his 1854 work, Walden

to gain true wisdom. But is not the reward worth the effort? If you have a Bible that includes the *Wisdom of Sirach*, I encourage you to read again the first six chapters, which often return to this theme. Meanwhile, here are a few selections -

> "My son, if you really desire to be a servant of the Lord, get ready for severe testing. Fix yourself on the true path, and stick to it, and learn how to stay calm and unmoved when things go wrong... Put up with every hardship that befalls you, and stay patient even in the hour of humiliation; for just as gold is tried in the fire, so the Lord will test all whom he has chosen in the furnace of contempt. ... Woe to you who have turned timid, and grown lazy. ... Woe to you faint-hearts who have abandoned your trust. ... Woe to you who have given up the struggle! What will you do when the Lord calls you to Judgment?... Wisdom exalts her children and always stands beside those who seek her. ... Those who get up early to greet her will never lack true joy. ... (But) she begins by making you walk first along a tortuous path, fraught with many perils, so that her discipline seems unendurable, and her demands impossible to meet. But when you have learned to trust her, then she will suddenly appear before you again, to show her sweetest secrets and bring gladness to your heart...
>
> "So then, my son,... lock your feet into wisdom's shackles, lower your neck into her yoke, bend your back under her load, and do not fret against her burden. ... When you have met her demands she will renew your strength, and transform herself into laughter. Her bonds will become your toughest protection, and her yoke your finest robe; her fetters will change into a golden ornament, and her chains into a scarlet sash. Then you will put her on like a glorious gown, and wear her like a garland of happiness!"

Thus we must impose upon ourselves the discipline of learning wisdom, and then instruct the people to do the same. This is the first part of the pastor's duty: to present his congregation with the word of God *explained.* But then he must advance, and bring them the scriptures in their second aspect, which is the *REVEALED WORD.* The next chapter takes up that theme.

Chapter Eight:

A PROPHET OF GOD

The second part of the true pastor's duty lies in bringing to his people

THE REVEALED WORD

Imagine an apostle praying for the churches he has founded. What is the theme of his prayer?

Surely he will cry to God for a great outpouring of the Holy Spirit, for a heaven-sent revival, for a mighty harvest of souls? We expect him to plead for many miracles of healing, for the blind to see, the deaf to hear, the lame to walk, the dead to be raised. No doubt he will seek wonderful answers to prayer for his people: for their financial needs to be met, for the funds to build a larger auditorium, for God to intervene in a thousand situations?

But wait!

We listen astonished. None of those things are in his mind. He gives no attention to the matters that constantly occupy our prayers. He ignores the things we beg for repeatedly and mostly in vain!

Then what *does* he pray for?

Read *Ephesians 1:15-20* and you will find out! In essence, his prayer was simple -

> *"Lord, give them a <u>revelation</u> of your word."*

Paul knew that their most urgent need was to get the blindness out of their spiritual eyes, and the deafness out of the ears of their souls. If they could but grasp inwardly the full measure of the riches and power that were available to them in Christ, everything else would inevitably follow. All the other things they might pray for would reflexively fall into their hands. They needed only the word of God to come forcefully *alive* in their hearts!

This became then a major thrust of Paul's ministry and of his prayers: not merely to bring *knowledge* to the people, but *revelation*. The same must be true of us. We have not done our duty until we have gone beyond *explaining* the scriptures to *implanting* them in the hearts of the people. The word of God must be changed from being merely a truth learned to a power experienced. The truth first grasped in the mind must now explode into energy in the soul. Only then do the promises of God become truly life-transforming in their effect, and the key to possession of all the treasures of divine grace and power.

> **The major function of prayer is to unlock the word of God**

Full exploration of what is meant by bringing people to the word *revealed* lies beyond my scope here; it is big enough to take a full book by itself.[95] So I am content simply to state the matter, and then move on to the next part of our duty as preachers, which is to proclaim the scriptures in their third aspect -

THE PROPHETIC WORD

One of the silliest questions I am asked from time to time is this: *"What is the Lord saying to the church?"* The focus, of course, is not on a particular local church (for then the question would be sensible), but on the church nationally, or even world-wide. But given the astonishing diversity of the church - in constituency, maturity, culture, affiliation, and many other things - it is absurd to suppose that the Holy Spirit could be addressing one message to the whole Body. Even within one denomination, within one city or state, the question is largely meaningless - except in very general terms.

Some things, of course, are demanded by scripture of all churches, such as: make disciples, establish holiness, train ministry, plant new churches, and the like. But beyond that mandate for the whole church everywhere, when the Risen Christ wished to speak a further word, he addressed it to individual congregations. Thus, in the letters John had to write to the *Seven Churches of Asia*,[96] Jesus gave a different set of instructions for

---

[95]   See for example, my books Faith Dynamics, Throne Rights, and Mountain Movers.

[96]   Revelation 2:1-3:22

each congregation. There is no reason to suppose that he acts any differently today. Are there a dozen churches in your area? Probably the Master has something distinctive to say to each of them, even if they are all part of the same fellowship.

Yet the church is plagued by the copycat syndrome: whatever works for my neighbor must work for me; whatever the Lord is saying to them, he must be saying to us. That seems so foolish. Almost certainly the Lord wants to say something that is unique to you and me in our situations, just as he did to the Asian churches.

Of course, it is much less troublesome, far less arduous, simply to pick up someone else's program than to seek out *God's* strategy for my locality. Indeed, many pastors find it easier to travel around the planet and attend a dozen conferences than to wait upon the Lord for divine instruction! Yet in the end, no plan will enable any of us to complete the work the Father has appointed, except his plan. That is the one, the only one, we should find and follow.

God seldom if ever repeats a strategy

When Israel marched out of the wilderness, across Jordan, and into the Promised Land, they had many cities to conquer, and territory to capture. Constantly they sought God for his plan of battle. Whenever they did so, they triumphed; otherwise, they failed.[97] They had to get God's maneuver for each new battle, because *God seldom repeated a strategy*!

Consider Jericho. There the plan was trumpets. But only once. God never again employed that tactic. If the Israelites had tried to capture any other city by blowing trumpets alone, they would have been massacred. Happily, they were wise enough to avoid that folly. Instead, the Lord brought them victory through an astonishing variety of ploys: the angel of death; the blinding cloud; cascading water; Moses' upheld hands;[98] clever ambush; crushing hailstones; disrupted planets; and angry hornets - along with the more normal hand to hand combat. Elsewhere in scripture, God made Israel triumphant by cacophonous thunder from the

---

[97]   One example from many, Numbers 14:44-45

[98]   Ex 17:8-13 plus these references, linked with the additional items above; Js 8:1,2; 10:6-11; 10:12-14; 24:12

heavens, a shattering earthquake, divinely induced panic, the sound of an invisible army marching, magically appearing pools of water, and other remarkable stratagems.

When David was captain of the Lord's host, seven times he *"sought the Lord"* without once receiving a repeated plan. Each time God had some new device, a different ruse to foil or overcome the enemy. Has the Lord suddenly lost his imagination? Can he no longer give us just the plan we need to bring us to the success he has ordained for us?

This is surely a vital part of the pastor's duty: to hear what the Lord of the whole Church is saying to each particular church. This is the special *prophetic* word a godly pastor must bring to the people from time to time. This is the leader's peculiar privilege in Christ: to discern the mind of the Lord, to gain *his* strategy for each ministry, to build just the church, and no other, that *he* has planned for that locality since time began!

> *"We honor God, because he keeps things hidden; we honor a king when he unravels them. ... Where a prophetic oracle is lacking, the people will do whatever they please; but blessed is the man who holds them to the way of the Lord!"*[99]

---

[99] Proverbs 25:2; 29:18.

Chapter Nine:

THE SACRAMENTS

The *practical* unity, fellowship, and worship of the church depend upon, cohere in, and arise out of the devout observance of the two major sacraments: *water baptism* and the *eucharist*.[100]

This becomes therefore a cardinal responsibility of the church overseers: to ensure that the sacraments are kept integral to the spiritual life of the church, and that they are observed with solemnity and faith.[101] This is the second part of the pastor's duty, after fulfilling the primary task of preaching the word of God.

> Roman Catholics reckon that there are seven sacraments: baptism; confirmation; the Eucharist; penance; extreme unction; holy orders; and matrimony.

> *Protestants* reckon there are but two sacraments: *baptism*; and the *Eucharist*.

Who is right?

It would take a braver man than I to give a firm answer to that question! But I will venture a few opinions, hoping they will not be too far from a true understanding of scripture.

The word "sacrament" does not occur in scripture. However, it is linked with the NT through the Latin word *sacramentum*, which was used to translate the Greek word *musterion*.[102] Unfortunately, *sacramentum* was not a good translation of *musterion*, and it introduced into the church ideas that go beyond the meaning of the Greek word. The apostles used

---

[100] 1 Corinthians 12:13; 10:15-17, 21-22

[101] 1 Corinthians 11:23,27-31. The note that follows, dealing with the sacraments, are substantially drawn from a chapter written by me in the book, The Church by Barry Chant published by Vision Ministries, Sydney. It is one of the volumes in the Vision Correspondence Course.

[102] Matthew 13:11; Romans 11:25; 1 Corinthians 2:7, Ephesians 1:9, 3:3-4, Colossians 1:26-27; etc.

musterion to describe God's great plan of salvation, which for many centuries was hidden, but is now made known to the church through the gospel. Scripture calls this plan a "mystery", both because it was hidden for so long, and because even now it can be discovered only by those who embrace Christ.

However, during its journey from *musterion* to *sacramentum*, the idea of "mystery" became attached not just to the gospel, but even more to the means by which the gospel was proclaimed in the church. The first of those means was, of course, the word. You can see the beginnings of the process that attached the idea of "mystery" to the word, in Ephesians 3:3-6 and Colossians 1:25-28. It was not long before the same idea began to be attached to any observance that revealed some aspect of salvation, or that created some kind of encounter with the risen Christ. The two most notable examples were naturally *baptism* and the *Eucharist*, but other things were easily included. Among them were

- *the laying on of hands (Hebrews 6:1-2);*
- *anointing with oil (James 5:14-15);*
- *even Christian matrimony (Ephesians 5:31-32).[103]*

Nonetheless *musterion* was not fully taken over by *sacramentum*, nor did it receive the kind of definitive or technical sense it now has, until almost the fourth century. In other words, for at least two hundred years the church did not sense any need to adopt a collective term to describe a particular group of its ordinances. If you had asked those early Christians whether there were two "sacraments", or seven, they would not have known what you were talking about. This suggests that the term "sacrament", as we use it, is artificial, and the quarrel about how many "sacraments" there are seems needless.

So then, against the Protestant contention that there are only two sacraments, another objection may be raised: the NT itself describes more than two agents through which the Holy Spirit reveals the mystery of Christ to the church. But then the Catholic list of seven sacraments seems just as arbitrary.[104] Why specify either two sacraments, or seven,

---

[103] Notice Paul's early use of Musterion in this reference.

[104] Unless of course it is claimed, as Rome does, that the church does have authority to make such lists and to impose them upon all its members.

when neither scripture nor the early church found it necessary to be so definite on the subject? The quarrel would vanish if the various antagonists would simply drop the word "sacrament" (with its hoary and largely unbiblical accretions), and return to the more open statements of scripture.

That seems an unlikely prospect. So we shall have to continue using the word. But first, we must decide what it means, and what things it belongs to.

Are the sacraments a "channel" or a "sign" of grace?

There are two main ideas about the meaning of "sacrament": that it describes a *channel* of grace; or, that it describes a *sign* of grace.

In the first view, the worshipper actually encounters Christ in the sacrament, and receives an infusion of the life of Christ - that is, the grace of God is conveyed to the worshipper through the sacrament.

In the second view, the sacrament has an exclusively symbolic or memorial purpose - that is, there is no conveyance of grace.

The peril inherent in the first view is that the sacrament may become its own focus, that the attention of the worshipper will be fixed on the sacrament, rather than on Christ, without whom the sacrament is void.

The peril inherent in the second view is the reduction of the sacrament to a perfunctory observance. It will then be stripped of any really useful or gracious function in the church, and made redundant to a full Christian life. Both perils have been too often realized.

Sacraments have no meaning apart from the word of God

Sacraments do not lie at the heart of the church. That place belongs to the word of God - see 1 Corinthians 1:17, 18, 21; Ephesians 5:26; Colossians 1:5-6; Romans 10:17; Hebrews 6:5; 1 Peter 1:23-25; Revelation 19:13; etc.

Clearly the word can and does exist without the sacraments; but sacraments have no meaning apart from the word. The sacraments exist only because the word commands them and gives them life. Again, the word is essential for salvation, so that since Adam not one soul has been saved apart from the word. The sacraments lack that grace.

Many people have entered the kingdom of God without them. Not that the word itself saves. Christ is the Savior. But Christ is made known through the word; hence the apostle did not hesitate to associate the word with the *musterion* of the gospel.[105]

Sacraments are most likely to become objects of magical superstition when the word is denied its pre-eminent place. So long as the church maintains the centrality of the word, no sacrament can be given an undue prominence, and the faith of the people will retain its proper focus - that is, it will remain fixed on Christ, whom the word alone clearly reveals.

Foremost in the church stands Christ; proximate to Christ is the word, revealed by the Holy Spirit and proclaimed by the messengers of God.[106] Then, and only then, come all the other ordinances in the church.[107]

To establish the primacy of scripture, it has been God's common practice throughout history to add certain attesting "signs" to his word. Those signs have been of two sorts: *ceremonial* and *supernatural*. They are given for a double purpose: to confirm the word *miraculously*; and to convey it *visibly* to the people:

♦ *confirming the word supernaturally is primarily the task of the charismatic signs; and*[108]

♦ *conveying the word visibly is primarily the task of the ceremonial signs.*[109]

I use the description "primarily", because the functions of the two groups of signs do overlap to some extent. In other words, the charismatic signs may provide a visible demonstration of the word in action, and a revelation of Christ, while still fulfilling their ordinary task of

---

[105] Cp. Ephesian 3:3-6; Colossians 1:25-28.

[106] Romans 10:8, 14-17 1 Corinthians 2:9-11.

[107] The psalmist expressing this supremacy of the Word in his striking exclamation: "You have exalted your Word even above your name!" (Psalm 138:2.)

[108] Cp. Mark 16:20; Hebrews 2:3-4 etc.

[109] Cp. 1 Corinthians 11:26; Hebrews 9:8; etc

supernaturally confirming the truth of the word. That is, they may preach as well as perform.

Likewise, the ceremonial signs may be a means of bringing the power of Christ supernaturally to the church, besides fulfilling their ordinary task of providing a visual picture of the message the word contains. That is, they may perform as well as preach.

The idea of "mystery" connects with both sets of signs: the <u>charismatic</u> (cp. *1 Corinthians 14:2*); and the <u>ceremonial</u> (cp. *Matthew 26:29* with *13:11*). Therefore the description "sacrament" may be applied to both sets, for God intended both of them to be a means by which the church could

♦ *enhance its fellowship with him;*

♦ *sharpen its vision of Christ;*

♦ *experience his life and power; and*

♦ *share in the drama of Christ's death and resurrection.*

> **A church without charismata must fall back onto ceremony**

Thus far we have traced the following development: the idea of "mystery" (or of sacrament) began with the divine plan of salvation; then it passed on to the word that revealed the plan; and then, because they are a means of proclaiming that word, and/or of conveying its power to the church, the charismatic and ceremonial signs also became identified with the "mystery".

Then something went wrong.

The charismata began to vanish from the church, leaving a vacuum in witness and experience that had to be occupied. That vacuum was filled by the ceremonies (notably *baptism* and the *Eucharist*), which became for many people the only possible source of the kind of supernatural experiences that had formerly been brought to them by the charismata.

But this obliged these ceremonies to support a burden much heavier than the one given them in the plain words of scripture, which in turn led to a further unfortunate development. Because the ceremonies had now become the prime means of realizing the word within the church, they were said to encompass the "mystery" of the gospel in a special way. That is, they took on a special character of "sacredness". They were thought of as belonging peculiarly to God. Thus the early Latin-speaking church changed *musterion* to *sacramentum*.

There is a subtle and emotive difference in the meaning of those two words. *Musterion* was originally used in secular Greek to describe the various "mystery" cults, along with their secret religious and political teachings. In the NT it means simply

> "the secret thoughts, plans, and dispensations of God,
> which are hidden from human reason... and hence must
> be revealed to those for whom they are intended" (Arndt
> and Gingrich).

In that sense, the word occurs more than 20 times in the NT, which applies it to many different things.

Sacramentum, however, originally meant "a deposit placed before the gods". Therefore it described an object that was reckoned specially sacred, being owned, as it were, by the gods, and therefore jealously guarded by them. A *sacramentum* possessed a uniquely divine quality. The word conveyed a more strongly sacrosanct feeling than did *musterion*. It induced a deeper sense of awe and reverence. That which Christians formerly valued, because it contained the "mystery" of the gospel, they now revered as an object "sacred" in itself.

Against all superstition we raise a vigorous protest

From the belief that certain ceremonies (or "sacraments") were highly sacred, and that they had a peculiar capacity to reveal Christ, it was a short step to the idea that these sacred ceremonies were themselves replete with grace. Even more, not only was grace deposited in the sacraments, but those sacraments could now cause grace to appear in the worshipper, without reference to that person's life. Unless the worshipper deliberately erected a mental or spiritual barrier against the sacraments, they would automatically convey the grace of God to him.

Thus the sacraments became sources of divine grace, independently of the word, and indeed soon surpassed the word in importance. They even began to usurp the place of Christ. The vision of a risen and glorified Christ became lost in the doctrine of a fleshly Christ, who was more or less imprisoned within the sacraments, and who was accessible to Christians only through those sacraments.

That sorry development was most observable in the celebration of the Eucharist during the Middle Ages. The priests, in the minds of a superstitious populace, became like magicians who possessed an awesome ability to change bread and wine into flesh and blood. The people believed that the priests even had power to control the unseen world, both supernal and infernal; they could command both heaven and hell.

Against such mediaeval superstitions the Reformers vigorously protested. They rightly insisted that the Holy Spirit cannot be controlled by any man, and neither does the grace of God yield to human command. They restored the biblical emphasis: sacraments exist to serve the word of God; sacraments have no validity apart from the word of God; sacraments are effective only when the participant is striving to obey God and believes the promise of God; sacraments belong to those, and only to those, who have established a personal relationship with Christ.

Such an insistence on true worship and faith is the one thing that can separate a genuine sacramental observance from one that is merely magical. The sacraments do not get their virtue from the various elements of water, wine, bread, oil, and the like, nor from priestly craft, nor from ritual actions. Their virtue comes solely from the salvific work of the Holy Spirit. He alone is the Conveyer of grace to all who participate in a sacrament, providing they do so with repentance, faith, true love, and sincere worship.[110]

However, even if we grant that the word and the Spirit are the true source of divine grace, the question remains: in what way, if any, do the sacraments provide a channel of that grace to the worshipper? And another question: which observances in the church should we call "sacraments"? In other words, how many sacraments are there, and in what way do they benefit the church?

---

[110] Romans 5:5; 14:17; 15:13,16; 1 Thessalonians 1:5; Titus 3:5; Hebrews 6:4-6; Ephesians 4:30; Etc.

Chapter Ten:

HOW MANY? HOW OFTEN?

My answer to the question about how many sacraments there are has already been partly given. It seems inescapable, from the broad way the scriptures use *musterion*, that there are several observances or practices, found both in public worship and in private devotion, that possess a sacramental quality (that is, they are somehow identified with the "mystery" of the gospel).

It also seems inescapable that the issue of whether or not they are channels of grace does not affect the matter of their number. In other words, if I believe that grace is channeled through one scripturally commanded observance, then it is not difficult to believe that grace can be channeled through all such observances - whether baptism, the Eucharist, laying on of hands, anointing with oil, or singing "psalms, hymns, and spiritual songs", and so on.

Likewise, any argument that can be used to deny a conveyance of grace by one observance (say, the Eucharist), is equally effective against all the others.

So, leaving aside for the moment the grace issue, and sticking to the NT use of *musterion*, it seems valid to say two things -

(1) There are several observances that may be called sacraments, but the number is probably indeterminate.

Thus Latourette, describing the church in the 15th century writes -

> "Much of the religious life of the laity centred in the sacraments... It was not until 1439 that their number was finally officially fixed. Some authors revered by the Church had spoken of only two: baptism, and the Eucharist. Peter Damien (11th century) had enumerated twelve, and Hugo of St Victor (12th century) thirty.

> "Peter Lombard (12th century seems to have been the first to limit them to seven and to give the list which the Roman Catholic church eventually made final."[111]

The same author writes elsewhere -

> "Before the year 500 the exact nature of the sacraments had not been given clear authoritative interpretation, nor had the number been fixed.

> "What there was in the Middle Ages which led to more precise official definition is not certain. Perhaps it was the prominence given the miraculous. After a discussion which lasted for several centuries, the number was officially decreed to be seven - by the Council of Florence in 1439."[112]

If the number of sacraments has to be set, after centuries of debate, by a decree of the church, clearly there is insufficient evidence to resolve the matter from scripture alone. Which means, if one is unwilling to accept that 15th century decree, the matter should be left unresolved.

The second valid thing we may say about the sacraments is this -

(2) Among those several observances there are two that scripture gives special prominence: baptism, and the Eucharist.

These two sacraments stand apart because they are uniquely associated with Calvary. In a way no other observance can imitate, baptism and the Eucharist present the passion of Christ. Other observances undoubtedly gain their value from the cross, but unlike baptism and the Eucharist they do not specifically portray Christ's death and resurrection.

Christ himself suggested this special link between his passion and the two major sacraments, by his enigmatic question to the sons of Zebedee -

---

[111] K.S. Latourette, A History of Christianity; Harper & row, New York, 1975; pg 528.

[112] A History of the Expansion of Christianity, vol 2, "The Thousand Years of Uncertainty"; Zondervan Publishing House, Grand Rapids, Michigan, 1970; pg 423

*"Are you able to drink of the **cup** that I shall drink of,
and to be **baptised** with the baptism that I am baptised
with?"* [113]

Most Protestants recognise as sacraments only baptism and the Eucharist, because those two have no meaning apart from their association with Calvary. In a powerful way they uniquely portray of the passion of Christ.

By contrast, other possible sacraments do not have that special identification with the cross. They may depend upon the cross for their validity, but they are not figures of it.

So without denying the possibility that other ordinances or practices may rightly be called sacraments, it does seem fair to place baptism and the Eucharist in a special category.

They can therefore be recognised as sacraments in a pre-eminent sense.

How often, and why?

Let me here focus on the Eucharist. Jesus gave this blunt command to his disciples: "This do, in remembrance of me"[114]

The way in which scripture expresses that command leaves no doubt that the Master expected the Eucharist to be a regular and constant practice in his church. The Apostolic Fathers had no doubt about that. As early as Justin Martyr, we learn that the churches held at least a weekly Eucharist-

> "On the day which is called the day of the sun there is an assembly of all who live in the towns or in the country; and the memoirs of the apostles or the writings of the prophets are read, for as long as time permits. Then the reader ceases, and the president speaks, admonishing us and exhorting us to imitate these excellent examples. Then we arise all together and offer prayers... both for ourselves and for... all men everywhere, with all our

---

[113] Matthew 20:22. KJV; see also Romans 6:3-4; 1 Corinthians 11:23-26.

[114] 1 Corinthians 11:24,25.

hearts. ... (Then) we salute each other with a kiss when we have ended the prayers. Then is brought to the president of the brethren bread, and a cup of water and wine. And he takes them and offers up praise and glory to the Father of all things, through the name of his Son and of the Holy Ghost, and gives thanks that we are deemed worthy of these things at his hand. When he has completed the prayers and thanksgiving, all the people present assent by saying *Amen*. ... When the president has given thanks and all the people have assented, those who are called deacons with us give to those present a portion of the Eucharistic bread and wine and water, and carry it away to those that are absent. ... We hold our common assembly on the day of the sun, because it is the same day (on which) Jesus Christ our Savior rose from the dead."[115]

A document that probably pre-dates even Justin gives similar teaching -

"Assemble on the Lord's Day, and break bread and offer the Eucharist..."[116]

From that time on, most Christian churches throughout the world have maintained at least a weekly celebration of the Eucharist. However, some evangelical and pentecostal/charismatic churches have minimised the spiritual value of the Eucharist, and have inevitably suffered spiritual loss. I find it dismaying to see pentecostal churches that once centred their worship around the Eucharist now treating it cavalierly - diminishing the frequency of their observance, or omitting it altogether if for some reason they deem it inconvenient.

Is this Table just a commemoration, or a communication?

Let me ask you: "Is this table just a commemoration of the passion of Christ; or does it bring a communication of the grace of God? What did Jesus mean when he used the term `remembrance'?"

---

[115] Apology, Bk I, ch 65-67; dated c. 150. Taken from Documents of the Christian Church; Selected and edited by Henry Bettenson; Oxford University press, London, 1973; pg. 66,67.

[116] "The Didache", ch 14; op. cit. Pg. 234.

Christians have given varying answers to such questions:

♦ *those who follow the Roman Catholic tradition argue that the bread and the wine actually become the flesh and blood of Christ;*

♦ *those who follow the Lutheran tradition argue that they convey the flesh and blood of Christ, while remaining unchanged themselves;*

♦ *those who follow the Calvinist tradition argue that they convey what the flesh and blood signify;*

♦ *those who follow the Baptist tradition argue that they are merely symbols, conveying nothing.*

In the idiom of Jesus' day, the phrase "do this in remembrance" meant "remember with a view to action" (see Psalm 25:6-7, plus many other examples). Therefore the expression will scarcely allow the baptistic view; this remembrance means much more than a simple recollection; it is more than just "calling something to mind"; it is a catalyst for divine action. We are bound to see a communication of divine grace in the Eucharist. But if that is so, who could be content with a careless, occasional, or indifferent usage of this holy gift? Who could ever weary of it? Surely the apostolic practice of at least a weekly Eucharist is the minimum we should allow.

Nonetheless, we cannot accept the view at the other extreme, that the officiating priest has power to transform the elements of bread and wine into real flesh and blood.

Both life and death are vested in the sacraments

Where then should we stand concerning the sacraments (both baptism and the Eucharist)? If churchly dogmatics and decrees are ignored, it seems wrong to believe either (a) *that the sacraments are symbols only, with no power to convey the grace of God to a worshipper; or* (b) *that they are supernaturally full of the grace of God, which is automatically conveyed to anyone who receives them.*

Surely scripture shows clearly enough that the power of God, both to heal and to destroy, is associated with the sacraments (1 Corinthians

11:27-32; 10:14-22; Acts 22:16; 1 Corinthians 6:11; Hebrews 10:22; etc.).

Yet it is equally plain that the sacraments do not have power merely because they are observed. Whatever capacity they have to convey grace to the recipient arises from two sources:

(1) the preaching of the word, which brings Christ to the people;

(2) a believing and worshipful response to that word by those who receive the sacraments.

> **Sacraments are powerless without the Word and the Spirit**

Without the word and personal faith, the sacraments are either rendered futile or become a channel, not of grace, but of divine judgment (1 Corinthians 11:27,30).

Those, then, who are baptised in trustful obedience to the command of Christ should expect to encounter the resurrection life of Christ as they emerge from the water. Their baptism should bring them into a new and higher dimension of Christian life (Romans 6:5-11; Colossians 2:12).

Similarly, those who celebrate the Eucharist should do so with repentance and faith, knowing there is a real presence of Christ at the table (in the bread and in the cup). Therefore worthy eating and drinking will convey to them the healing grace of Christ (1 Corinthians 10:16). [117]

But we should allow no one to imagine that he or she can observe any sacrament carelessly. Where there is neither repentance nor faith, the participant should expect nothing from God except wrath (cp. Jude vs. 11-13). No sacrament has any inherent power to save anybody. Salvation comes from Christ, who gives it only to those who receive and believe his word (1 John 5:6-12). Sacraments have power only when the Holy Spirit acts in and through them to convey divine grace to those who

---

[117] Note however, since scripture make no attempt to explain in what way Christ is present in the eucharist, or in any other sacrament, neither do I. Let the dogmatists argue about it if they will; but I am content to remain as silent as the scripture is on that subject.

through the sacraments show their confidence in the word and their love for Christ.[118]

We conclude that a true pastor will ensure that his people are well taught in the biblical doctrine of the sacraments, and he will insist that the sacraments are observed with sobriety and faith.

---

[118] Let me say also that the grace channeled through the sacraments is not some special sacramental grace, different from any other. It is the regular grace of God that springs out of Calvary. The sacraments are simply special channels of that grace, a special means by which that grace can be conveyed to the worshipper. It is however, possible that they do add to that grace a dimension, which may not be so readily available from some other source.

Chapter Eleven:

KEEP THEM HOLY, NOT HAPPY

Something outrageous creeps across our land. The church, against which the gates of hell should beat in vain, has pusillanimously yielded to the character of this world. God's roaring lion has been tamed, and now mews like a domestic cat. Everywhere two worldly syndromes can be observed:

> *(1) Churches have meekly succumbed to the world's opinion that their existence must be justified by offering a package of services to the community.[119]*

What a spectacle! A pitiable church driven to apologize for being there. A Christian congregation striving to purchase community acceptance by its good deeds - as though it had no better reason to exist than some secular organization. So church leaders, though lacking a divine mandate to do so, commit themselves to various enterprises - daycare centers, schools, counseling services, programs to feed the hungry, or clothe the naked.

No doubt such programs do reflect Christian concerns, and show the compassion commanded in scripture; but they would be better done by groups of qualified lay people than by the church acting as a corporate entity.[120]

We have no need to explain ourselves to anyone, nor to justify our ministry to man or devil. We are here because *God* has put us here. We are here whether they love us or loathe us. We are here to preach Christ and make disciples; and we will do it, whether they want us to or not. And while they may destroy us individually, they cannot destroy the church - it is Christ's own building, and it will stand for ever.

---

[119] Such as counseling services, schools, childcare centers, welfare activities, youth programs, recreational and sporting facilities, educational opportunities and the like. Such things may all be good, and acceptable to God; but often the underlying reason for them is a desire to gain a respectability in the community often at the price of severe compromise.

[120] See my further comments on this below.

So then, whatever the church may choose to do in the way of good works or community service, must never be done merely to prove its right to exist. No project should be tolerated that diminishes its prime duty of bringing people to maturity under the full lordship of Christ. We require no other reason to exist than obedience to the mandate of Christ. We have not been sent to please our neighbors, but to *evangelise* them; not to keep them comfortable, but to *disciple* them; not to make them happy, but to make them *holy*; not to encourage their greed, but to teach them *self-sacrifice*.

> *(2) Churches have tamely accepted the market mentality of the surrounding culture. That is, they have adopted a policy of creating whatever package will attract the most customers, no matter what it costs in loss of discipleship.*

Consequently, many churches now measure "success" by the same "bottom line" criteria that control their secular commercial neighbors: statistical growth and profitability. Where can that be found in scripture? How can it fit the teachings of Christ who promised a sword not peace, and that we should be hated not loved, scorned not admired, and cursed not praised? He did allow that the ungodly might sometimes *"speak well of us"*; but he at once gave a warning: when they do so, *"Beware!"*[121] The church faces its greatest threat when the world begins to honor it!

No doubt we should strive to live peacefully with all our neighbors[122]. Nonetheless, something inherently perilous for the church lies in the applause of this world; something is deeply wrong with a church that is hungry for secular approval, or craves wide popularity.

If you are a Christian pastor, what is your true task? After preaching the word and administering the sacraments, it is to establish discipline. *That is, to turn* converts *into* disciples.

Our task is not to make them happy, but holy

Whatever gave the church the idea that our task is to make people happy, to solve their problems, to keep them prosperous and contented, to make their lives pleasant? When Christ called me into Christian ministry, he

---

[121]   Matthew 10:17-23; Luke 6:26

[122]   Romans 12:18.

didn't send me to make friends, but to make disciples. My commission was not to hand out good advice, but to preach the gospel. I have no duty to entertain the people, but I am obliged to admonish and correct them.

In a word, the pastor's job is to get people out of hell and into heaven - anything that lies outside that task should hold no great place in his interest.

Call to mind Jesus' injunction about "plucking out your eye, and cutting off your hand"? [123]

In his reckoning, it was better to go maimed into heaven than whole into hell. He was not too worried about whether they were crippled physically, but strongly insistent that they should be sound spiritually. Their earthly life might be one of frustrating disablement, but that had little importance so long as their heavenly destiny was secure.

Unlike their Lord, many pastors are busy sticking "hands" and "feet" back onto people, when they should be encouraging them to cut off a few more. The shepherds have changed their role. They work so hard at creating a pleasant, untroubled life for their people, trying to keep the congregation happy, *they have forgotten how to make them* holy.

> **It worked for your neighbor, but it may not work for you.**

Here is an example of what I mean. Suppose a church is thinking about establishing a child-care center, or a pre-school. What are its reasons? Perhaps to generate income, to contact unconverted families, to help families where both spouses are employed outside the home, or to build better relationships with the neighborhood. But are those valid reasons? The question at least deserves to be asked, and a more careful answer given than pastors are prone to offer. Some pastors have no better reason than this: the idea worked for a neighboring church, and so ought to be worth copying. That is not good enough. We ought to do nothing, except what God has specifically mandated for our ministry or church.

The real task of the church is simple: nurture the souls brought into its care by the witness of its members, and bring those souls safely into

---

[123]   Matthew 18:8-9

heaven. Nothing more is needed for that task than the proclamation and enforcement of the word of God. Anything else is extraneous to that true work, and may well be deleterious to it.

Possibly the Holy Spirit has instructed a certain congregation to set up various additional programs. If so, those programs presumably will fulfil everything expected of them. But does that same mandate apply to every church? For one church to copy what another has done may create two problems:

first: such programs usually fail to add any significant number of souls to the kingdom of God, despite enormous expenditure of finance, energy, and time; and

second: they tend to become dominant, like a tiger held by the tail - you soon discover it was a mistake ever to grab it, but now you dare not let go! So these activities tend to consume all but the largest churches, yet they are hard to get rid of after they are started. Hence many local churches, when they begin some kind of community project, find themselves, like Jonah, being swallowed by something bigger than they are. And the monster keeps getting ever more voracious.

So then, if a church starts a school, pre-school, welfare center, clinic, and the like, they may grow into the dominant part of its ministry, absorbing most of the energies of its staff, and most of its finances. Programs to feed the hungry, clothe the naked, serve the needy, and the like, are prone to overwhelm the proclamation of the gospel under a mass of bureaucracy. Church leaders should ask: is that what we want; can we prevent it from happening?

> **Does happiness come from stuffing**
>
> **a house with possessions?**

An even more subtle problem can be created by projects like a pre-school: what message do they send to the community? Some churches will find that their outreach, far from teaching spiritual values, actually endorses the secular goal of a self-indulgent lifestyle.

How many families in your suburb really need both parents to work, except to maintain an artificially high standard of living? If they were content to live in a humbler home, to drive a cheaper car, and to dispense with some extravagant entertainment's, perhaps most of those families could manage well enough on one income. Should we not be teaching them to do that, in obedience to the gospel, instead of encouraging them to devote half their labor and income to luxuries? (1 Timothy 6:6-11). Should the church be encouraging people to think they will be happy only if they can stuff their home with more and more possessions? [124] Even pagan philosophers have known better than that -

"I need a jug of wine and a book of poetry,
     Half a loaf for a bit to eat,
Then you and I, seated in a deserted spot,
     Will have more wealth than a Sultan's realm."[125]

Are you content for your church to preach a poorer ethic than an agnostic mediaeval poet proclaimed?

Yet many pastors are so enmeshed in the caring ethic of this world that they have allowed themselves to become just a small cog in a vast secular health and welfare apparatus. They have unwittingly adopted this world's philosophy: the ultimate good in life is earthly happiness based upon good health and material prosperity. To achieve that end, says society, any expense is warranted, no effort is too great. Thus a huge part of our government's budget is devoted to curing every human ill, and to protecting people from all pain. That may be, and no doubt is, an admirable goal for politicians, but it is less than commendable in pastors. Why should we even *seem* to be endorsing the deadly illusion that the best life is free of suffering, that the highest aim of men and women should be their own health and happiness? Should preachers of righteousness be encouraging people to focus more of their attention upon this life? Have we no higher call than to achieve for ourselves and for our hearers a comfortable, pleasant, pain-free life on earth? Rather than playing an insignificant part in this world's struggle to remove all pain and to sanitize death, should we not rather concentrate upon what

---

[124] The ideas expressed above, dealing with pre-schools, are based on an article in Christian century" magazine, March 15, 1989. I have lost the magazine, and have no further details of the article.

[125] The Ruba'iyat of Omar Khayyam, quatrain #98; Avery, op. cit. Pg. 71

only we can do: help people to discover the redemptive power that lies even in the dark valley of the shadow of death?[126]

Am I wishing upon others what I could hardly endure myself? No, for like you, I am not eager to suffer, nor to be poor, and I hope to continue enjoying good health and prosperity. If I should take sick, I would ordinarily utilize every skill of modern medicine to ameliorate misery and bring recovery. I am grateful for our hospitals, medical staff, clinics, pharmacies, and the like. To be otherwise would be absurd.

Nonetheless, I am a pastor not a physician, a preacher not a counselor, a shepherd not a nurse. There are others in the church for whom the role of visitation, of comfort, of nurture, is more proper. I cannot allow myself to be called away from the truly necessary merely to do the important.

Furthermore, I am a Pentecostal pastor, which means that I do pray for the sick, and have seen some astonishing miracles of healing. But still my ultimate thrust is not physical, but spiritual healing; and not freedom from tears in this world, but happiness in the next. Any lesser goal is delusory.

Let some business-people do it, not the pastor

"But," someone may say, *"we are catering for the single parent!"* Are you really? How many single parents (especially mothers) can afford pre-school fees? Your unintended result may instead be to create resentment among your own people. Their tithes and offerings built the pre-school, but many of them cannot afford to send their own children there. The same might be said about a Christian school, when it is owned and operated by the church. The student fees are often beyond the reach of parents in the congregation.

So the pre-school, and the school, may become primarily a "service" the church provides for the affluent. Instead of confronting the well-to-do with a demand to live more simply, to practice self-denial, to take up the

---

[126] The thoughts in this paragraph are based upon my recollections of an article in The Christian Century. By William H Williman. I would have quoted it directly except that the passage was inadvertently wiped from my computer, and I have no other details of it.

cross and follow Christ, the church supports their insatiable quest for more luxury. That might still be acceptable if the enterprise resulted in bringing them to repentance. But in fact few of those prosperous people will ever express any interest in the righteous message of the church. Why should they, if the church by its own action is undermining some of the deepest principles of the gospel?

Once again, there may be good reasons for building a child-care center.[127] Those reasons may be valid and God-honored. Perhaps the Lord himself has given approval for such a project.

Even so, the task would still probably be done better, not by the church itself, but by a separate body of capable lay people. The pastor should encourage a group of business people to form their own corporation, to raise their own finance, and to manage it themselves. Keep such projects off the church property. Keep them away from the church itself. Let nothing intervene between the church and the righteous word it is called to proclaim. Let nothing blur the sharp focus of the church upon the gospel. God has made the church competent in only one thing: building his spiritual kingdom. The church should stick to that task. Let someone else do the rest.

Any project whose result is to siphon the energies and finances of the church away from its biblical task of bringing men and women to holiness under the absolute lordship of Christ, is probably out of God's will. Material success alone is not sufficient to turn aside that judgment.[128]

---

[127] Or a day school, or hospital, or clinic, or welfare program, or any other community-service project.

[128] Fiscal or statistical success is no necessary sign of God's favor. If that were so, we would have to say that the great international corporations of our time are enjoying more divine prosperity than any church has ever known! Clever pastors, without God's help, may create highly successful enterprises (in a material sense), only to find on the day of Judgment that the Lord saw them building nothing but worthless sandcastles (cp Matthew 7:26-27; 1 Corinthians 13:1-3).

I can't solve everyone's problems!

I wonder why so many pastors think they are competent to solve everyone's personal problems? Have they been to university? Do they have a degree in psychology? Are they registered counselors? Would they try to supplant the physician, and offer people medical advice? Do they imagine themselves bankers, seeking to straighten out everyone's personal finances? Are they mechanics, able to repair every broken machine? Then why do they arrogate to themselves the role of counselor, posing as qualified psychiatrists? What right do these amateurs have to pontificate on every mental, emotional, and relational problem of the troubled souls who come to them for help?

When a sick person calls for a pastor, should he start prescribing medicines? Or should he rather preach Christ the Healer, lay hands on them, and pray for them in Jesus' name, asking for a miracle of healing?

When someone in financial distress cries out to him, should he play the banker and start delving into their affairs? Or should he rather preach Christ the Provider, lay hands on them, and pray for them in Jesus' name, asking for a miracle of supply?

If those prayers for healing for some reason do not suffice to make the sick well, should he not advise the sufferer to see a physician? If those prayers for prosperity for some reason do not relieve the bankrupt's distress, should he not advise him to visit a financial expert?

It is deceitful for a pastor to claim a competence he does not possess, to pretend to an expertise he cannot ratify.

When someone comes to me with personal problems I have no remedy to prescribe except Christ the Savior. The gospel is the only medicine I am competent to administer. If for some reason the sufferer is unable to seize the joyous victory Christ offers, I am not going to pretend to a skill in counseling that I do not have. I will instead send him or her to someone who, by long and arduous study, has qualified himself or herself to offer sound advice to those who seek help.

Stick to things in which you may truly claim competence

I am willing to share scripture with anyone, and to pray with them; but if for some reason prayer is ineffective, or if their problem is other than a spiritual one, I refer them to someone who is professionally qualified in their area of need - whether a physician, lawyer, financial advisor, counselor, or psychiatrist. In common with most pastors, my skill lies only with hurts that are likely to respond to a spiritual remedy. We should stick to things in which we may reasonably claim to be competent, which truly fall within the orbit of our call in God. But some pastors are like the know-it-alls Sei Shonagon spoke about sourly a thousand years ago -

> "A man who has nothing in particular to commend him discusses all sorts of subjects as though he knew everything."[129]

This was Jesus' psychology: if your hand offends you, cut it off!

Jesus set a better example. He had nothing to say except what belonged to the gospel. He refused to play the counselor for a man who sought his advice. He would not allow himself to be imposed upon. He had no interest in solving that man's fiscal and relational problems.[130] Probably he reckoned himself unqualified to adjudicate such matters. Anyway, he was unwilling to do so. He had a higher priority than satisfying human greed and selfishness. His eye was not on earthly affairs, but on the kingdom of God. Indeed, he had a neat method for solving personal problems: "if your eye offends you, pluck it out; if your hand offends you, cut it off!" *Jesus was not much into psychology.*

---

[129] Morris, op. cit. pg. 44.
[130] Luke 12:13-15.

Chapter Twelve:

DISCIPLINE MAKES A CHURCH

Paul would not have polled well in any popularity contest. His counseling technique, like that of Jesus, was too blunt and brutal -

> *"I hear that some of you have disputes with each other. ... This is my opinion of your quarrels: if you must argue about such trifling matters, then take the most ignorant and the least important person in the church, and make him your judge. I say this to make you ashamed. ... The truth is this: by going to law against each other you show that you are already utterly defeated. Why not rather allow yourself to be robbed? Why not let yourself be defrauded? Instead (by going to law) you turn yourselves into cheats and frauds - and you do this against fellow Christians!"[131]*

Pastors should follow the example of Christ and Paul, and not make themselves accomplices in human selfishness and self-centredness. The church does not exist to indulge the craving people have for what they think are their "rights". We are here to preach Christ and to call them to holiness. Indeed, if you are a pastor of a church, that is probably all *God has called you to do, and all you are* gifted *to do. But then, what nobler duty could you possibly have? Why should you allow yourself to be enticed away from the highest task to the lesser one of solving personal problems? Why should you make yourself the servant of earth-bound aspirations, of temporal happiness, of worldly treasure, when your real work is to turn the eyes of the people heavenward?*

Our task is not to hand out good advice,

but to preach Christ

Pastors, therefore, should not diminish themselves into cheap sources of professional and (unless they are trained) probably unreliable counsel.

---

[131]   1 Corinthians 6:1-8

So let me ask: are you truly trained, qualified, and experienced as a counselor? If not, you may do more harm than good if you try to unravel someone's tangled life by stepping down to the level of good advice.

> ## Don't shift from the preacher's pulpit
> ## to the counselor's couch

There is more vainglory than good sense behind the glib assumption of skill some pastors make, especially if they are still young in ministry. Profound knowledge, long experience, thorough training, are needed to cope with complex and horrendous human needs. No doubt any pastor (no matter how inexperienced he may be), if he sticks to scripture and to the revelation of Christ, is *highly capable of helping people. But when he shifts from the preacher's pulpit to the counsellor's couch he often becomes a tragic mistake waiting to happen.*

For the ordinary pastor, trained only in scripture, the rule is sound: cling to the ministry of the word and to prayer. [132] If you must step outside that boundary, then do so reluctantly, cautiously, with a sense of peril. If people are unwilling or unable to accept help from you within a strictly gospel framework, then you would generally be wise to send them off to a properly qualified professional. If they have to pay for it, they may take the counsel more seriously. Perhaps also, if professional counsel fails them, they may be driven to offer a full surrender to Christ! He will then at last be able to do his own work in them!

> ## Is there a problem that scripture does not bluntly call sin?

I do not mean that people cannot come to me with any problem they like. They can and they do. But I do mean that I have only one answer, no matter what problem they bring: Christ and the gospel. *They will hear nothing different from me across the coffee table than they hear from the pulpit. If they won't heed scripture when it is proclaimed under the anointing of God in church, why should I expect them to receive it when I tell them the same thing in private?*

---

[132] Acts 6:2

117

But whether or not they want to hear it, that is all they *will* hear, in secret or in the open, in season or out of season. As a preacher of the gospel all of my ministry finally comes down to one message: repent, believe the word of salvation, and start living under the true lordship of Christ! *I doubt if anyone has ever brought me a personal problem that scripture in one way or another does not call sin.*[133] Somewhere all those grievances have their roots in the flesh. Professional counselors, psychotherapists, physicians, can treat the surface effects, and do it well; but only Christ has power to penetrate the soul and bring healing where it is most truly needed.

Consider Paul: he had no interest in knowing more about *himself*; he wanted to know more about *Christ.*[134] He had no desire to placate the old nature; he put it to death in Christ! It is impossible to imagine him spending many hours and repeated sessions, exploring the wounded childhood's, the wretched environment, the terrible upbringing, the ghastly circumstances, the harsh poverty, the twisted psychology, of the whores, thieves, murderers, drunkards, homosexuals, squalors, liars, lechers, rogues and other assorted misfits who comprised many of his converts.[135]

No doubt they had enormous personal problems. But he didn't call their hurts "problems", he called them sins, which had to be abandoned at once, and cast aside by faith. He had the same remedy for all of them: put off that old nature; re-clothe yourself with Christ; walk as God's new-made man and woman! If that were not adequate for them, Paul had no other solution to offer.

Repent! Or drop dead!

Peter, it seems, believed in the same principle; although in one case, the story of Ananias and Sapphira, it had a terrible outworking.[136] How

---

133 See the wide range of things Paul castigates as "works of the flesh" in Ephesians 4:17-32; Galatians 5:19021; Colossians 3:5-9; 1 Corinthians 6:9-11; etc.
134 Colossians 1:9-12.
135 1 Corinthians 6:9-11; Colossians 3:5-9; etc.
136 Acts 5:1-11

would you handle a case of deliberate falsehood in the church? I'll warrant, not the way Peter did!

Nowadays, the expected thing would be a private counseling session, followed by kindly and sympathetic admonition. You would surely begin with a gentle exploration of why the two people had made such a bad choice. You would want to find every possible mitigating circumstance. Then you would work on a quiet rectification of the problem, and of course make a strong effort to keep the couple in the church as active (and giving) members.

How harsh Peter's reaction seems to our tender sensibilities, and how offensive to modern views on the rights of the individual.

Surely he could have been a little more tolerant? Is there no room for Christian mercy, for sympathetic understanding, for pardoning love? How poorly Peter met those *demands!*

Surely it would have been better, more fruitful, more glorifying to God, if he had taken the couple aside privately, calmly shown them their error, and then taught them higher principles of honesty? Did he have to *kill* them? How can you build a big church if you destroy people whenever they make a mistake? A more kindly approach might in time have turned them into beautiful Christians.

Peter plainly didn't know much about modern counseling techniques! Which is fortunate, for if he had, and the apostles had abandoned gospel advocacy for good advice, where would the church be?

Note that the first mention in *Acts* of the word *"church"*, is in this story! If the hermeneutical principle of "first mention"[137] applies here, then we may be meant to understand that the scattered crowd of new converts were not truly bonded together into God's "ecclesia" until after this event. The exercise of divinely wrought discipline began to turn them into disciples.

---

[137] That is, the first mentions of a subject in scripture often determines its basic meaning thereafter.

If your aim is evangelism, be honest enough to say so

The apostolic approach seems strongly contrary to some of the prevalent ideas of our time, among which is the motive that underlies many local church counseling ministries. The argument goes: if we can reach out to people, solve their problems, and make them happy, then they will surely join our church. It seems to me that two problems are created by that concept -

(1) An ethical distortion corrupts any claim of caring about people, when the real aim is evangelism.

The announced intention of the project is to meet the need of hurting people; but the hidden purpose is to add them to the church. That is not honest. The church should walk in the light of Christ, not deviously, not using subterfuge to trap the unwary.[138]

The same kind of warp occurs when preachers exploit the attendance of unbelievers at a wedding or a funeral, and assault them with the terrors of hell. That is an intolerable rudeness. Only the courtesy and better manners of the crowd prevent such ungracious preachers from getting the black eye their tactless words invite.

There is a proper time for everything, including a time to speak up, and a time to keep quiet - even about the gospel.[139]

True love has no need to operate under a pretence, nor to employ a hoax. If you plan to preach the gospel, if your aim is evangelism, then say so. Give people the same freedom God gives them, to decline to listen to you. You have no right to impose yourself upon a captive and unwilling audience.

The second problem is akin to one discussed in the previous chapter -

(2) By turning themselves into problem-solvers, pastors encourage people to think that their personal health, happiness, and prosperity are the most important things in the world.

---

[138] 1 John 1:5-7
[139] Ecclesiastes 3:1-8; especially vs 7.

The people have responded to this environment by changing their expectations of their pastors. God's shepherd is no longer seen as a man devoted to holiness, prayer, and preaching, but as a Jack-of-all-trades. The renowned novelist, Taylor Caldwell, once made this acid comment on the issue of people learning to live simply so that their pastors might live godly -

> "Man does not need to go to the moon or other solar systems. He does not require bigger and better bombs and missiles. He will not die if he does not get better housing or more vitamins... His basic needs are few, and it takes little to acquire them, in spite of the advertisers. He can survive on a small amount of bread and in the meanest shelter...
>
> "His real need, his most terrible need, is for someone to listen to him, not as a patient, but as a human soul. ...
>
> "Our pastors *would* listen - if we gave them the time to listen to us. But we have burdened them with tasks which should be our own. We have demanded not only that they be our shepherds, but that they take our trivialities, our social aspirations, the "fun" of our children, on their weary backs. We have demanded that they be expert businessmen, politicians, accountants, playmates, community directors, "good fellows", judges, lawyers, settlers of local quarrels. We have given them little time for listening, and we do not listen to them either. ..."[140]

The task of the church is simple: nurture the souls in its care, and bring them safely to heaven. That task is based upon one act: the proclamation and enforcement of the word of God. Anything else is probably injurious to its true fulfillment.

---

[140] From an article in "The Listener"; quoted in The Art of Understanding Yourself, by C. G. Osborne, Zondervan Publishing House, Grand Rapids, 1973; pg. 10-11

Where discipline is lacking, holiness will fail

I am pressing this idea upon you: our God-given task is not to make people comfortable and prosperous, nor to rid their lives of difficulty, but to *"make disciples in all nations"*.[141]   A necessary part of making *disciples* is the practice of *discipline*, which is required from the leadership in every local church.[142] A lack of courage in this matter, a reluctance to act firmly and decisively against outrageous conduct, has encouraged many people (including some fallen pastors) to continue boldly in sin which has brought great scandal upon the church.

Circumstances may prevent churches from adopting other programs, but discipline is possible in every environment, whether a congregation is small or large. However, this does expose a weakness in big churches. Since the personal lives of most of the people remain unknown to the pastors of the church, effective discipline becomes impractical. In a smaller congregation faulty behavior cannot be so easily hidden, and can be dealt with appropriately. Of course, that does not always happen, and occasionally it is the larger church that raises the standard of holiness unto the Lord.

Nonetheless, whether a congregation has many people or few, if discipline is absent it is presumptuous for it to claim to be a true church. As Clement of Alexandria said nearly 1800 years ago -

> "For the most part, that goodness which is always mild is despised; but he who admonishes by the loving fear of righteousness is reverenced."[143]

Without discipline you only have an audience, not a church

Paul had no doubt about where his duty lay: he was able to express it clearly, simply, forcibly. As a guardian of the church, his one all-consuming task was to present it to Christ as "a pure virgin Bride". *And he knew how to achieve that goal -*

---

[141] Matthew 28:19-20.

[142] See Matthew 18:15-18; Romans 16:17-18; 1 Corinthians 5:1-5, 9-13; 1 Thessalonians 3:10-15; etc.

[143] The Instructor I.ix; Anti-Nicene Fathers Vol 2. Pg 231b.

*"Without fear or favor we admonish each of you,
preaching Christ to you, teaching you the way of
wisdom, so that everyone may realize their full potential
in Christ."[144]*

If this apostolic pressure were to be exerted in some churches today, their
congregations would be decimated overnight! Some pastors, in the name
of holding a big crowd, tolerate rampant self-indulgence, contentions,
carnality, half-heartedness, even downright immorality. Can their big
audience rightly claim the holy designation, "church"? It doesn't have to
be that way, of course, and there are large churches where holiness *is*
insisted upon, just as there are smaller ones that shun any discipline. But
regardless of size, any congregation that wants to meet the criteria for a
"church" will have to obey the rule -

*"Strive with all your heart to be holy, for without
holiness no one will see the Lord."[145]*

An unbiblical feminising of the pulpit is happening

Another reason why there is confusion in the church about its proper
role, and why perplexed pastors are breaking down, is this: church
leaders do not know whether the pastor's duty to the church is to be its
"father" or its "mother", or both. That is, a tension in Christian thinking
arises from the contrast between the "fatherly" role of the "bishop" (the
senior leader of the local congregation) and the "motherly" role of the
church.

Scripture describes the church in feminine terms, as the "Bride" of
Christ. Consequently, her collective role is the motherly *one of
compassionate nurture of souls.*

The "bishop", however, is the direct representative of Christ the
Husband. Therefore he is described in masculine terms, and his role is
the fatherly *one of admonition and discipline.*[146]

---

[144] 1 Corinthians 11:1-3; Colossians 1:28.
[145] Hebrews 12:14.
[146] See again our major text, 2 Timothy 4:1-5.

Across most of Christian history those two roles have been at least covertly recognised, and kept apart from each other. That is why the office of pastor has had a strongly masculine cast, which has made it unappealing to most women.

But in our time, a radical change has occurred: the role of the pastor has been feminized. His dominant function is no longer that of instruction and rebuke, but of tender pity and gentle succor - as though his work is motherly, not fatherly. Now he is expected to console, *not discipline; to* counsel, *not admonish; to* comfort, *not exhort. Consequently, men are abandoning the ministry, and their place, in several great denominations, is increasingly being taken by women. This inevitably feminizes the pulpit still more and makes it even less attractive to men.*

Am I opposed to women in ministry? Do I dislike a woman preaching? Am I against female ordination? Not at all! There is ample room in the church (and in scripture) for a gifted woman to serve God in whatever capacity the Lord has appointed for her. Indeed, because some women make better "fathers" than "mothers" (just as some men are more motherly than fatherly)[147], there is no reason why they should not be the senior pastor of a church. But that is uncommon. Most women are motherly, most men are fatherly; to force either into the opposite role is to compel them to behave against their basic nature.

Therefore, in the ordinary purpose of God, the "bishop" will be a man. He must reflect the commanding authority of Christ in the church, a function that few women can fulfil comfortably. Anyhow, whether occupied by a man or a woman, the pulpit must normally speak with a fatherly not a motherly voice. If it becomes feminized, then strength and holiness in the church will certainly be diminished, and perhaps destroyed.

The fatherly and motherly roles must both be present

The church is not a business corporation, but a family; therefore it functions, not around the impersonal dynamics of a secular corporation, but around the personal dynamics of loving relationships. Like a broken

---

[147] Note that these terms have nothing to do with "manliness" or "womanliness", or even with "maleness" or "femaleness". I am not talking about gender, but about temperament, personality, and gifting in God.

family, the church becomes dysfunctional unless both the masculine and the feminine characteristics are found in its ministry. The church itself should provide the feminine; the "bishop", the masculine.

Here is a law of life: the motherly role can function under the fatherly; but the reverse is not true. If the motherly becomes dominant, the fatherly will vanish. By its very nature the motherly heart is gentle, pitiful, and tender. If it is the ruling voice in the church, it cannot tolerate the fatherly actions of stern rebuke, firm correction, and unyielding discipline. But the fatherly can readily tolerate, in fact welcome, the exercise of the motherly role under the protection of its strength and discipline.

Because most women are not fitted for a fatherly role, they have not in the past been attracted to a ministry that required it. But now the reverse is occurring. The motherly aspect of Christian ministry is becoming dominant, and men who are not fitted for that role find the pastor's task unappealing. They look at the modern pulpit and what do they see? Sound doctrine is disliked, discipline is abandoned, rebuke is no longer accepted, preaching must be kindly and pleasant. The key word is no longer righteousness but benevolence; divine compassion has been replaced by human sympathy; friendly advice is expected, not bold declaration, and even less, stern admonition.

The result? The pastor is not a prophet any more, but a counselor, a problem-solver, a helper, an advisor. The pulpit becomes feminized; and the more this happens, the less attractive Christian ministry will be to most men.

So the congregation should be instructed on how to fulfil its nurturing, mothering role as the Bride of Christ. But God's "bishop" has a different function, a stricter, tougher one, enforcing righteousness, demanding holiness, carrying the church firmly on toward maturity in Christ.[148]

Whether you are a man or a woman, if God has called you to be the head of a local church, you should understand this, and resist the current pressure to "feminize" your task. Refuse those who want you to accept the motherly duties of compassionate nurture in place of your true fatherly task of instruction and discipline.

---

[148] 1 Timothy 3:1-7; Titus 1:5-9.

You should cast off the role of counselor, of amateur psychiatrist. Where does scripture command a "bishop" to be a practical advice-giver, a personal problem-solver, a prescriber of recipes for happiness? Leave those nurturing tasks in the hands of secular professionals, or to qualified people in your church. Then commit yourself to your proper task: preach righteousness; demand holiness; impose discipline; build the kingdom of God.

Proposition three:

WORK –

"Labor to spread the gospel"

Chapter Thirteen:

AUTHORITY IN THE CHURCH

Thomas Carlyle once wrote -

> "Cannot one discern too, across all democratic turbulence, clattering of ballot-boxes and infinite sorrowful jangle, needful or not, that this at bottom is the wish and prayer of all human hearts, everywhere and at all times: *`Give me a leader; a true leader, not a false sham-leader; a true leader, that he may guide me on the true way, that I may be loyal to him, that I may swear fealty to him, and follow him, and feel that it is well with me!'* The relation of the taught to the teacher, of the loyal subject to his guiding king, is, under one shape or another, the vital element in human Society; indispensable to it; perennial in it, without which, as a body reft of its soul, it falls down into death, and with horrid noisome dissolution passes away and disappears."
> [149]

In that dramatic passage Carlyle points to the weakness of democracy, and also highlights the human craving for strong leadership. It is a phenomenon everywhere observable. Thus, walk past almost any checkout in any large American supermarket, and you will probably see at least one magazine cover featuring a member of the British royal family. The Queen and her kin are as popular - perhaps more so - in the USA as they are in the United Kingdom! This adulation of royalty probably has at least some root in a yearning desire for the kind of strength and stability that democratic republicanism can never provide.

The same principle is true for the local church: if strong leadership is absent, then the whole body, as Carlyle said, will "fall down into death." [150]

---

[149]   Chartism, ch. 6. (written in 1839)
[150]   Compare Ecclesiastes 10:16,17.

But leadership depends upon *authority*; therefore the question must be asked: *"Where does ultimate authority reside in the church?* With the pastor, the eldership, the people, the denominational managers, or somewhere else?"

> **There are four human models of authority, and one divine**

Across the ages, *four* governmental models have dominated human societies. From time to time various churches have also adopted those same models. They are -

MODELS OF AUTHORITY

(A) THE SOCIOCRATIC MODELS

(1) Four governmental models have dominated human society -

(a) Anarchy - the lack of any rule

There are still churches that allow no one to have authority over the individual believer. They permit only the *quietist* or *illuminist* principle of being "led" solely by the Holy Spirit. Any sort of form or structure is denounced as "carnal" or "worldly".

(b) Autocracy - rule by one person

Autocratic authority exercised by one powerful lord has been the most common shape of human government. The various kinds of "episcopal" or hierarchic structures in the church all reflect an autocratic pattern. Such churches claim that the rule of Christ, the Chief Shepherd, must be expressed through several ranks of under shepherds (pope, cardinal, archbishop, bishop, priest, and the like).

(c) Oligarchy - rule by a few

From the consuls and triumvirate of ancient Rome to modern troikas, this too has been a frequent model of government. In the church the various forms of "presbyterian" rule follow the oligarchic principle. By their reckoning, the authority of Christ resides in a council of elders.

(d) <u>Democracy</u> - rule by the many

Here, the church has been a leader rather than a follower. Modern democracies are all indebted to the democratic principles established 400 years ago in the various Reformation churches that adopted a "congregational" form of government. They argued that the rule of Christ in the church is best expressed through the collective will of his people. They refused to place substantial authority in the hands of one man, or in any clique of men, but only in the full company of the saints.

(2) None of those four models is adequate for the church, the Body of Christ. Corruption too easily overtakes each of them, thus turning

"anarchy" into chaos.
"autocracy" into tyranny.
"oligarchy" into privilege.
"democracy" into paralysis.
- which forces us to a different model:

(B) THE THEOCRATIC MODEL

The ultimate and only Lord of the church is Christ, and none can usurp his authority. Authority in the church, therefore, does not flow *up* from the grassroots, but *down* from the throne of heaven. The purpose of this chapter is to examine the practical outworking of this model in the local church.

Authority does not flow up from the people,
but down from God

Someone might protest that a "theocracy" will soon become the same as "anarchy", with each person doing whatever he pleases while claiming that he is not depending upon himself but rather upon personal guidance from heaven.

Indeed, that is what happened in Israel, which found that a theocracy is easy to establish but difficult to maintain![151] Churches have had the same problem, so they tend to fall back upon one of the other four models.

---

[151]   Judges 21:25.

But in the end, again like Israel, they pay dearly for that decay of the divine ideal!

How can we set up and maintain theocratic rule in our churches?

Scripture shows that God always channels his rule through *delegated authority*, and in doing so he embraces elements of each of the other kinds of government. Hence we can say that a theocratic church will be

(1) Organic

The biblical picture of the church is one of a *charismatic organism*, not that of a *controlled organization*. Hence the development of a monarchical episcopate, the suppression of the charismata, the smothering of enthusiasm beneath regimented forms, the creation of structures that negate control by the Holy Spirit, the placing of authority entirely in the vote of the laity, and so on, have all become heavy impediments upon the true vocation of the church.

Anything that compromises the theocratic nature of the church will frustrate its missionary mandate. No matter how intrinsically good such things may be, they must be rejected.

(2) Pragmatic

The lack of a clear paradigm in the NT suggests that the churches are free to work out the principles of the theocracy in any practical way they can. Therefore they should structure themselves in whatever way is most conducive to maintaining life and witness within a given culture, while remaining always within theocratic parameters.

(3) Autonomous

This means, of course, *self-governing*. Scripture shows that each local church was a self-contained unit. Why? Because only the local overseers, and the people with them, can reasonably discover the mind of Christ for their church and their community. Nonetheless, the local church should not be *independent* so much as *inter-dependent*, and its autonomy is subject to three modifiers:

- *the rule of scripture*, for no one inside or outside the church has the right to countermand the ultimate authority of God's inspired word.

- the restraints of fellowship, which should lead all churches and ministries to consider not only the effect their actions will have on themselves, but also on others in the larger communion.

- the recognition of ministry, which should make us respectful of those spiritual leaders whom the Lord has plainly anointed and given, not just to one church, but to the fellowship of churches.

(4) Hierarchical

A modified episcopacy, functioning within the local church, and perhaps within a group of local churches, seems the most biblical structure. This concept argues that authority in the kingdom of God is *monarchical* not *democratic;* that is, it flows *down* from the King, not *up* from the people. For this reason, the ministry-gifts of the ascended Christ[152] are not necessarily limited to one local congregation. Depending upon the call of God, they may be exercised over companies of churches, which are also apparently free to band together into district or regional groupings.

The Chief Shepherd and the Under-Shepherds

So we could say that the kingdom of God contains a hierarchy, which incorporates aspects of *each of the other four forms of government.* This is because God always channels his rule through *delegated authority.* If so, then we should view the structure of the church as follows -

(1) Christ, the Chief Shepherd - theocratic rule

The absolute Lordship of Christ over his church is asserted in many places, among them *Hebrews 13:20; 1 Peter 5:4.*

(2) The Minister, the Under Shepherd - monarchic rule

♦ *This would usually be one person, whom by custom we call the pastor; but it can be expressed through a collegiate structure.[153] However,*

---

[152] Ephesians 4:11-13

[153] Secular powers have also experimented with collegiate rule, with mixed success. Note the ancient Roman Triumvirate, and the later sharing of

♦ *since authority vested in one man may easily become tyranny (1 Peter 5:3), and*

♦ *since scripture commends the wisdom found in a group of counselors (Proverbs 11:14; 24:6), and*

♦ *since there are diverse gifts and ministries in the body of Christ (1 Corinthians 12:14-27), therefore*

♦ *the senior pastor/bishop/minister is required to work with*

(3) The Overseers, the Lesser Shepherds - oligarchic rule

This is the next layer of leadership in the church, under the ruling minister. But notice that these presbyters/elders/councilors/deacons, must finally remain themselves under the absolute lordship of Christ, not of the ruling minister. Once again, no-one in the church has ultimate control except Christ. Thus the elders and deacons will eventually have to answer to Christ, not to their pastor, for the manner in which they fulfil the task the Lord of the church has given them.

We see then that Christ has delegated his authority in the local church to a combined group of under-shepherds (*Acts 20:28; 1 Corinthians 16:16; Ephesians 4:11-12; Philippians 1:1; 1 Thessalonians 5:12-13; Titus 1:5; Hebrews 13:17*; etc.). Therefore the full oversight of a local church, or of a group of churches, should consist of a plural eldership comprising the senior minister/pastor/bishop working in close co-operation with the elders/presbyters/deacons.

This collective leadership, when it is functioning as God intended, has a potential of immense spiritual power (*Matthew 18:18-20*). The authority the overseers possess in Christ is forceful, and in all matters relevant to the spiritual life of the church, to its mission and growth, its discipline and order, their rule must be honored by the people.

The exercise of spiritual authority by the shepherds should be marked by the following qualities

power by the emperors (two "Augustii" with four "Caesars").

- *strength (Hebrews 13:17; Acts 20:28)*

- *humility (1 Peter 5:2-4)*

- *vulnerability*

By "vulnerability" I mean that they should always be open to hear the voice of God speaking through a single member of the congregation, or through them all. God is not obliged to work only through the "official channels". Thus there is yet a fourth level of authority in the church, found in -

(4) The People, the Priests of God - democratic rule

See *1 Peter 2:5,9; Revelation 1:6; 5:10; 20:6; Acts 2:16-18; Hebrews 10:19-23; Romans 5:1-5; Hebrews 4:16.* Those scriptures declare the royal priesthood, the spiritual dominion, the privilege of full and free access to the throne of God that absolutely belongs to every believing man or woman.[154]

God is not bound to channel his grace through the pastor, or elders. He may choose instead to work his will through the people (either collectively or individually), to whom godly leaders should always give ear. Here is a lesson that some pastors could learn to their benefit, as the following story illustrates -

> "King Arthur had been hunting a stag, which after a long chase had escaped him. Weary and thirsty, he rested beside a spring of water, and fell into a strange dream-like state. It was a day with a spell cast on it, a day when reality is distorted like a reflection in disturbed water.
>
> "The king, dosing fitfully, saw several dark and troubling visions, and then it seemed to him that a boy approached him. As he watched, unsure whether he was awake or asleep, the child spoke, and began to talk about things that Arthur had thought hidden from all but himself. Angered by this, Arthur sent the child away. But then an old man drew near, and asked, `Why are you

---

[154] For a full study of this theme, see my book <u>Royal Priesthood.</u>

sad?' And the king replied, 'I am sad and puzzled by many things past, but just now a child came to me and told me things he could not and should not know.' 'The child told you the truth,' said the old man. 'You must learn to listen to children. He would have told you much more if you had permitted.'

"Arthur cried out, 'Who are you?' 'I am Merlin the old man. But I was also Merlin the child, to teach you to pay heed to everyone.'"[155]

Have we now explored all the levels of authority in the church? No, for there is still one more principle of government, one more expression of command, which is found in

(5)   The Saint, the Servant of God - anarchic rule

Sometimes the least significant person in the church may be the only one who sees the vision of the Lord. Notice the anarchy implicit in Paul's instruction in *1 Corinthians 14:30*. Anyone may receive a word from God, a prophetic oracle - and the apostle obliges the church to be silent and to give ear to it.

Consider also the daring of *1 John 2:27*, a verse that scratches most unpleasantly at the hide of entrenched dignitaries, who think themselves indispensable to the church!

The time sometimes arrives when one man or woman, against the advice and will of all, may have to stand alone, true to his or her own conscience. That is a dread time, for it is a frightful thing to stand alone against all one's friends and counselors. But in that hour, when the solitary spirit knows it is right, while the others are wrong, the brave heart must obey God rather than men.

Sirach understood this. He knew that only a fool would begin any important task without seeking the best wisdom; but he also knew that sometimes clear vision rests only in the eye of one person -

---

[155]   Adapted from a re-telling of the Arthurian legend by John Stienbeck, The Acts of King Arthur and His Noble Knights, Heineman, London, 1976; pg. 46-49

"Who would begin a great project without careful discussion? Who would take significant action without seeking wise counsel? Yet you must learn to trust your own judgment also, for which counselor will consider your interests better than your own heart will?

"Indeed, sometimes out of your own spirit there arises a word that is more trustworthy than the cry of seven watchmen standing on a high tower! Yet above all, keep on praying to the Most High, for only he can finally keep you walking on the right path."[156]

CONCLUSIONS

(1) Each local church should devise a structure that preserves all the above elements.

(2) Normally, final authority must remain with the oversight of the church, and ultimately with the senior minister, who is responsible under God for the welfare of the church. The varying levels of spiritual maturity in any growing congregation, make it impractical to rest the destiny of the church upon some kind of popular majority vote.

(3) The *pastoral* authority of the shepherds, and the *priestly* authority of the people, merge to form the *spiritual* authority of the entire church. That authority, when it is functioning truly, makes the church invincible (*Matthew 16:19; 18:18-20; Ephesians 2:19-22*; etc), and it gives to the church the right:

♦ *to preach the word of God*

♦ *to ordain pastors, elders, deacons*

♦ *to minister the saving grace of Christ*

♦ *to heal the sick in Jesus' name*

♦ *to discipline recalcitrant members*

♦ *to celebrate the sacraments*

---

[156] Sirach 37:16, 13-15.

♦ *to overthrow the kingdom of darkness.*

That is the kind of church we should be striving to build.

Chapter Fourteen:

MOBILISING SOULWINNERS

When the overseers of the church fulfil the three duties I have described above, in the *word*, the *sacraments*, and *discipline*, then the congregation will be fitted to fulfil the great task Christ has given to the church as a whole: EVANGELISM. But before a local congregation can fully obey that divine commission, it too must do three practical things:[157]

♦ *identify those in its number who have been especially gifted by God to win men and women to Christ;*

♦ *devise programs that will enable those people (whether lay or clergy) to fulfil their role; and*

♦ *mobilize the remainder of the people to serve God in their particular capacity or calling.*

One way to help each member of a congregation find his or her proper place, is to reduce all the various ministries and offices in the church to *four major functions*: evangelist; shepherd; exhorter; servants.

But first, here is an illustration of the principles upon which I have built this study.

Many years ago I worked as the accountant of a group of furniture stores in the suburbs of Melbourne. The firm had at least a hundred other employees. Some of them worked as shop sales people; others sold on commission from door to door; others drove trucks, packed the goods, repaired damaged items, and so on. Then there were the handful of us who worked in the administration building.

---

[157] They are based on the principles expressed in Romans 12:3-8, 1 Corinthians 12:28-31 and other similar passages.

I was employed there for over a year, during which time I never once saw any of the shops, nor a single item they sold, nor even one customer.

How did that happen? Simply because my job was upstairs in the accountant's department, in a separate head office building. The nearest shop was miles away from where I worked. So ledgers, journals, accounts, and countless columns of numbers engaged all my attention. Yet no one in the organization was any more committed than I to the success of its primary business, which was to sell domestic furniture and hardware to the citizens of suburban Melbourne.

How to ruin a business: make everyone sell!

Now imagine this scene. Suppose the owner has called all his workers into his office to rebuke us for declining sales. "The task of this business," he roars, "is to sell goods. A downturn in our profits cannot be tolerated. I want our sales turnover doubled in the next few weeks. All of you drop whatever you're doing, and get out onto those streets and *sell, sell, sell!*"

So we all down tools - clerks, drivers, packers, mechanics, bookkeepers, typists, shop assistants - and off we go to join the commission agents, cold canvassing the streets of Melbourne, trying to persuade reluctant customers to buy our goods!

If such a thing were to be done, what do you suppose would happen to the business?

You know the answer: swift chaos and total ruin!

True, the success of the enterprise did depend upon constant growth in its sales. But there was only one way to achieve that goal: each employee had to do well just the job he or she was employed to do.

In my case, that meant balancing the books of account to the last penny each month, which was done. There was no need for me ever to see a customer or sell a chair. Indeed, I would have harmed the corporation, not helped it, if I had abandoned the job in which I was skilled (accounting), and had taken on a job for which I was ill-suited (commission selling).

Of course the story is silly. No owner in his right mind would do anything so foolish. To find such ridiculous behavior in real life you have to visit the church, where you can see it constantly!

We are all involved in soul-winning;

we are not all soul-winners

The task of every Christian is to make disciples for Christ. That is the business of the church, and in the end it has no other. But that does not mean we must all be immediately involved in the task of "selling" the gospel to men and women. We cannot all take on the job of persuading reluctant "customers" to accept the offer of salvation. Some are called to that task, and skilled in it, while others are not.

Just as all the employees of that group of furniture shops had their particular role to play, so in the church each believer has a different function.

Let me change the illustration.

Paul likened the church to the human body. It is one body, but it has many different members, each of which has a unique function. Think about *your* body. When do you call it whole, healthy, flourishing, fully reflecting the image and purpose of God? Only when it has all its parts, and they are all functioning in the right place, in the right way, at the right time.[158]

The same must be said about the church: it cannot be healthy unless its various members are in their proper place, doing just what they are equipped to do. I have never yet met a preacher who does not give at least lip service to that analogy. We all agree with Paul -

> *"If the whole body were only one limb, what kind of body would it be? As you well know, we all have many different parts, yet we each have only one body. ... In a similar fashion, the church is Christ's body, and each of us is a limb or an organ in it."*

---

[158] Romans 12:3-8; 1 Corinthians 12:12-31.

Yet many of those same preachers and spiritual leaders, who teach enthusiastically that the church is the "body of Christ with many diverse parts", *in practice zealously ignore their own teaching. They feel compelled to force every member of the church to conform to a particular model of Christian life or ministry:*

♦ *thus one insists that all believers must be constantly involved in a program of personal soul-winning;*

♦ *another demands that every true saint must take on a burden of intercessory prayer;*

♦ *another declares that we must all abandon our selfish life-styles and merge into Christian communes, pooling our goods and incomes;*

♦ *another pressures every Christian to be deeply involved in pastoral care, reaching out to heal their hurting neighbors; and the like.*

Were we to accept all the burdens, duties, tasks, responsibilities that some earnest teachers want to impose upon us we would need days of 50 hours, and weeks of 50 days!

It is time not only to believe the doctrine of one body with many parts, but to practice it! Just as the "members" of our physical bodies have different, distinct, and non-interchangeable functions, so each person in the "body" of Christ has a particular place and task.

That raises an obvious question: what is your place, and mine, in the "body"? Let me answer that by summarizing the various offices and ministries in the local church under four headings[159]

---

[159] Note: in this study I am not dealing with the five ascension-gift ministries of Christ listed in Ephesians 4:11, but simply with the various ministries/offices/functions that should be occupied by the leaders and members of each local church. The "ministry gifts" conform to these functions, but usually reach beyond a merely local church setting

EVANGELISTS - A Ministry of WITNESS

Definition: an evangelist is a person gifted by God to persuade men and women to yield to the gospel of Christ.

Notice the verb "persuade". Any donkey can bray on a street corner, harassing passersby, rudely thrusting oneself upon the unwilling, bailing up the unready. That is not evangelism. I doubt also that any genuine love for the strangers they are annoying motivates such people. They show more sign of being driven by some kind of guilt. They behave like they are struggling to prove something - either to themselves or God - about their courage, their merit, or their piety. They are driven more by pangs of conscience than by a godly call.

A true evangelist does more than merely witness; he or she wins the lost to Christ. Christ did not command us simply to witness to all the world, but to make disciples in every nation. Therefore evangelism (that is, successful soul-winning) is a specific gift. There is no more reason to force every Christian to be an evangelist than there is to make them all apostles, prophets, pastors, teachers, administrators, or anything else. Indeed, if I may use the old version of Proverbs 11:29, only the wise can win souls, and that wisdom is itself a gift of God.

Therefore, since each believer has his or her proper function, the church should not try to force every person into a program of active evangelism. Rather, it should create opportunities, at various levels, for those who are true soul-winners to function - in house meetings, street evangelism, over the pulpit, mass crusades, and the like. Some soul-winners are gifted in one-on-one evangelism; others function effectively only when preaching to a crowd; some are skilled in both areas.

Find the people whom God has called to this ministry of witness; encourage them in it; open doors for them; but leave the rest of the church alone! A business that is all sales people will fail! A body that is all mouth is a monstrosity![160]

---

[160] Nonetheless. Scripture requires all of us to be ready at all times to share the gospel with anyone who enquires about it (1 Peter 3:15)

SHEPHERDS - A Ministry of WELFARE

> Definition: a shepherd is a person gifted by God with a special ability to heal the flock of Christ.

Although it should be obvious that this is not a role every Christian can comfortably fulfil, some leaders still try to make it mandatory for all their people to be involved in pastoral work. They challenge every family in the church to open their homes to the naked, the hungry, the broken. But for some families, that would be a recipe for disaster. They have neither the emotional nor spiritual resources to handle the stresses that would be caused by bringing hurting people into their homes.

I have seen families torn apart because one spouse, driven falsely by conscience, insisted on turning a house into a hospital.

Notice the terms in the definition above.

There are few people who meet those criteria, even among the most godly saints. Those who do qualify can hardly help themselves; you will always find them surrounded by life's orphans, showing the loving nurture of Christ himself.

There are three expressions of this shepherd role in the church -

(1) Counseling

Much harm has been done to both pastors and people by failure to recognise two different kinds of counselor -

> (a) those who provide short-term care

These are people with an amazing empathetic skill. Within a few minutes of meeting someone they have demolished the barriers we all build around ourselves, and torn to shreds the camouflage we all wear. They barely know your name before they are penetrating deep into your soul! They easily persuade you to tell them your most hidden secrets, to disclose your very heart, to place your naked soul under their healing touch.

But the very gift of these shepherds becomes their chief weakness.

After a few weeks of ministry people begin to resent the shepherd's growing intrusion into their private lives. They want to peel him (or her) off their souls; they want to escape the shepherd's hunger to have them dependent upon him; they want to stand free and whole as their own person in Christ. Unless the short-term shepherd can be moved aside, and turned toward new clients, conflict and pain will grow, and much of his or her good work will be undone.

Short-term shepherds are wonderfully gifted to care for new converts, or those who have recently joined the church; but after a stated period of time, the task of nurture needs to be taken up by

(b) those who provide long-term care

These shepherds are slower to form bonded relationships, and they do not penetrate so deeply into the minds of the people they nurture; but they are more likely to form life-long friendships, to make people dependent upon Christ (rather than upon the shepherd), and to sustain their ministry indefinitely.

Short-term and long-term counselors are seldom interchangeable. They each have a particular nurturing function.

By identifying among its people those whom God has called to this ministry of pastoral care, whether on a short- or long-term basis, the church should be able to establish a nurture program that will involve every member. None should fall by the wayside, un-noticed, uncared for, forgotten and forsaken.

(2) Curing

These are people in the church who are singularly gifted by God, either with supernatural gifts of healing (the charismata, 1 Corinthians 12:9-10), or with a deep heart of compassion for the sick and an urge toward and skill in nursing them back to health. Some may focus mostly upon simple physical illness; others may be more gifted in curing spiritual or mental afflictions.

(3) Caring

These are people large in hospitality, sympathetic, generous, friendly, who delight in giving hospitality, who display their love for Christ by caring for the practical welfare of anyone they meet who is hurting or needy (Romans 12:8,13).

From the above you can see that shepherds are marked by special qualities of empathy and compassion, which may not exist so richly in people who are called to the third major ministry in function -

EXHORTERS - A Ministry of WORDS

Definition: an exhorter is a person gifted by God to impel the church toward perfection in Christ.

There are three expressions of this ministry in the local church -

(1) Intercessors

You might wonder at my description of exhorters as a ministry of "words". Surely evangelists and shepherds also depend upon words?

Yes, they do; but with this difference: for an evangelist or a shepherd, words are a necessary means to an end, whether of conversion or wholeness. But for an exhorter, words are their own end. Once those words have been spoken, the exhorter's work is done. For example, consider a person whose gift is intercessory prayer. *The burden of the Lord drives him to his knees; he cries out to God; he persists in prayer until he knows he has prevailed. At once he is relieved of his burden, his labor is finished, he knows his words have triumphed and there is nothing more for him to do.*

Note that like all the other functions in the church, this too is a particular call, requiring special gifting from God. No one can appoint himself or herself to be an intercessor. This must be a God-given task, or it will fail.

(2) Prophets

Similarly, a prophet, having spoken the oracle of God, has fulfilled his commission. That was all God required of him, or her. It now rests with the people to whom the oracle was given to respond to it in whatever way they please. That is not the prophet's responsibility. His or her task was sufficiently done the moment the word of the Lord was spoken.

Once again, let it be clearly understood that prophets are called, not made. Only God can set a prophet (or any ministry) in the church (Ephesians 4:11).

(3) Teachers

Some who possess the ministry of an exhorter express it primarily through preaching and teaching. Like the two former expressions of this gift, these people also are content simply to speak the words God has given them. Once they have delivered the message of God to their hearers they feel satisfied; there seems nothing more for them to do.

Unlike an evangelist these people have little motivation (or skill) for altar calls (that is, for demanding an immediate response). They feel no obligation to press home a challenge for action.

The young man Elihu[161] provides a good example of a teaching exhorter. Like Elihu, these exhorters

♦ *yearn to bring people to maturity, and believe that can best be done by planting in them sound doctrine;*

♦ *have confidence in the power of words alone to accomplish the divine purpose for their ministry;*

♦ *believe that the words they have spoken can be trusted to continue working in the lives of the hearers;*

♦ *are satisfied by the act of speaking alone, believing that any further action on their part will probably disturb, not enhance, the effectiveness of their words*

♦ *will return to the theme again and again, however, if they do not gain a satisfactory response.[162]*

Many exhorters are frustrated by the "altar-call" syndrome of our time; that is, the pressure always to follow a message by some appeal for immediate action. At least in respect to their own ministry, they tend to view altar calls as at best superficial, at worst manipulative, and almost always detrimental to the real work of the Holy Spirit.

---

[161] Job 32:18-22. This use of Elihu as an example of an exhorter is not original with me. I came across if many years ago in a now-forgotten magazine article

[162] Job 33:1-2; 34:1-3; 36:1-2.

Exhorters are not sellers. They feel no need to "close the sale" by pressing for an immediate decision. They prefer to plant the seed of the word, and then back away and allow the Holy Spirit to water that seed and to bring it to fruition whenever and however he pleases.

Exhorters are a vital function in the church, for The Great Commission *commands us to make, not just* converts, *but* disciples.

The fourth ministry-role in the church is one that is often neglected, and yet holds importance in its mission. It is the work of those who are

SERVANTS - A Ministry of WORKS

> Definition: a servant is a person gifted by God to bring the church to organizational coherence in Christ.

This servant role is vital, for there can be no prosperity without it. There are two kinds of servant (1 Corinthians 12:28) -

(1) Administrators - "power to guide"

These are people gifted by God to see the organizational needs of the church, and to devise plans that will enable it to achieve its goals. They may serve the whole church, or just a single department.

Here is an essential ministry, which should be better recognised. Pastors dream dreams and see visions; but who will bring those heavenly musings into earthly reality? God-given administrators have the skill to see what collective structures, what practical stratagems, what kind of leadership and participation, will be necessary to implement the goals of the church.

I have seen a young pastor build a congregation up to a hundred or so people, upon which he realizes that he needs to employ an assistant. Instead of hiring a capable administrator, he mistakenly brings a clone of himself onto the church staff; that is, another pastor, a man with similar gifts and aspirations. At once a competition arises between them for pulpit time, for the allegiance of the people, for leadership authority, and the like. The new pastor becomes an adversary instead of an assistant. The process is almost inevitable, and could have been avoided by employing someone whose gifts were complementary to those of the senior pastor instead of competitive with them.

(2) Helpers - "ability to assist"

In this category belong musicians, choir masters, secretaries, treasurers; and so on. These are not inferior roles; their improper use can ruin the church.

For example, it is a mistake to appoint someone as treasurer just because he or she has some secular qualification as an accountant or bookkeeper. God's economy runs on different principles to those that govern this world! You do need a skilled treasurer, who can manage the books well. But much more, you need a treasurer who knows how to speak a word of faith into every financial situation, a treasurer who is more obedient to scripture than he is to the accountancy text book. Any other kind of person will put a strangling noose around the finances of the church, a cramping wall around its prosperity.

The same applies to musicians. People should not be appointed to this position merely because they are skilled performers. You don't need people who only "perform" music; you want musicians who "prophesy" through their music-making. David discovered that principle, and allowed no one to perform in the temple unless they were able to blend a prophetic sound with their music-making -

> "David... appointed as worship leaders certain of the sons of Asaph who were able to give leadership through inspired _prophecy_, using lyres, harps, and cymbals. ... (They were) under the direction of Asaph, who himself _prophesied_ by authority of the king. ... Jeduthun (also) _prophesied_ with the lyre, expressing praise and worship to the Lord... All these men were (appointed) to make music in the temple of the Lord... they were all _trained_ and _skilled_ in how to make music for the Lord"[163]

How much we still need such skilled and prophesying musicians! These are technically capable people who are sensitive also to the moving of the Holy Spirit, so that every note they strike resonates in harmony with the purpose of God. Never too loud, or too soft; never too fast, or too slow. Each melody reflecting the proper mood of the meeting at that moment, whether cheerful or sad, majestic or pensive, solemn or joyful.

---

[163]   1 Corinthians 25:1-8

I would rather be led by a one-finger picker whose every note has an echo of prophecy, than by a keyboard magician whose pyrotechnics dazzle the ear but leave the spirit unmoved.

Church leaders, then, should be careful about whom they appoint to one of these "servant" functions in the church. When the wrong people are placed in these offices, even the most gifted pastor may find his purpose constantly thwarted, and a spiritual dearth falling upon his church.

If what I have said above is true, then we are led inescapably to certain conclusions, which are taken up in the next chapter.

Chapter Fifteen:

KNOW YOURSELF

I am aware that there is always something artificial about any attempt to lock people into certain categories. They usually refuse to conform. No matter how firmly you try to box them in, arms and legs keep on sticking out all over! So I am not trying to limit the possible functions in the church strictly to the four I have given in the previous chapter: *evangelist; shepherd; exhorter*; and *helper*. Bracketing the ministries in this way is simply a device to clarify our view of the subject. Plainly, those functions may and do overlap, and could be described in other ways. Nonetheless, you will probably recognise yourself in one of them. That recognition may be helpful for determining your main role in ministry, and also the proper function in the church of other people in your congregation.

Notice also that any of the four functions may operate at various levels. That is, some will span the entire church, or touch only one department, or even only one family at a time. Some will be restricted to a single church, others will extend to a regional, state, national, or even international level.

Whether there are only four functions, or many more, whether they stand alone or overlap, they create a responsibility for each Christian and for the church -

First: there is the responsibility of the individual

Each member of the church should know his or her proper place in the body, and have the courage and faith to commit themselves to that role, refusing to be coerced into a different office or ministry, or bullied into taking on some task to which God has not called them.

The first counsel we should all accept is: *Know thy God!"* But the second is close to it in importance: *Know thyself!"[164]*

---

[164] According to Plato, this saying originated with the (continued on next page)

Here then are four rules for a balanced life -

(I) DON'T DEFLATE YOURSELF. HAVE THE GOOD SENSE TO KNOW YOUR STRENGTH, AND TO USE IT

Some Christians are unhealthily humble. They are reluctant ever to push forward, to take action, to put to use the talents the Lord has given them. Paul was bolder -

> *"Since we all have different gifts, according to the grace God has given us, let us USE them, right up to the limit of the faith we have received."*[165]

There is no room there for supine, passive piety! Use your talents, urged Paul. Stir yourself to action. Be up and doing! As the renowned Charlie Chaplin once said -

> "You have to believe in yourself, that's the secret. Even when I was in the orphanage, when I was roaming the streets trying to find enough to eat, even then I thought of myself as the greatest actor in the world. I had to feel the exuberance that comes from confidence in yourself. Without it, you go down in defeat."[166]

One important thing is missing from that saying: Mr Chaplin was able to see himself as "the greatest actor in the world" only because he recognised within himself a performer's skill. He could not so easily have imagined himself as the world's greatest concert pianist, or portrait painter, or novelist. But even allowing that he was innately a great actor, still nothing would have come from it without unwavering confidence. He truly did have to believe in himself, and he had to seize every opportunity when it came his way. Those dynamics remain unchanged in the church.

You are a man or woman in Christ. Through your natural birth, through the new birth, and through Holy Spirit baptism, you have received certain gifts and strengths from the Lord. Rise up in faith. Know who

---

(continued from last page) "Seven Wise men" of antiquity (c. 600 B.C.) It was also inscribed on a wall of the oracle at Delphi

[165] Romans 12:6

[166] I have lost the source of this quote

you are, what *you have, and with abounding confidence go out and* be *and* do *all that the Lord has placed within you. That is the secret of success with contentment. Either to fall short of it, or to go beyond it is to woo disappointment.*

(II) DON'T INFLATE YOURSELF. HAVE THE GOOD SENSE TO KNOW YOUR WEAKNESS, AND AVOID IT.

There are some things you will never be, things that will always lie beyond your achievement in the church and in your ministry. Be gracious and humble enough to accept those inbuilt limitations. The *"all things"* you can do in Christ[167] are no more than those things the Lord has appointed for you.

We must all live with limitation. Most things in this world lie beyond the grasp of even the greatest among us. Furthermore, very little in our character is susceptible to radical change. What you have been you are, and what you are you will be. Can an Ethiopian change his skin? Can a leopard scrub away its spots?[168] That is, can someone change their basic identity? No; even the most radical transformations that are wrought by the gospel usually alter no more than surface characteristics. Extroverts and introverts, phlegmatics and mystics, peacemakers and warriors, retain their temperaments. Despite an occasional repetition of the "Balaam's Ass" syndrome, where the inarticulate speak like angels, people are born with a particular identity, and must stay with it all their lives.

Many thinkers have made similar observations over the years. Here is just one example, from a perhaps unlikely source: a crime story, featuring Agatha Christie's Belgian detective, Hercule Poirot. A young woman, Lynn Marchmont, has come back from the war to find she no longer loves the rustic farmer to whom she is engaged to be married. Instead she feels attracted to a rival suitor, David. She laments the changes the war seems to have made to so many people -

"(Lynn) cried out:

---

[167] Philippians 4:13. Remember that Paul wrote this letter while he was in chains, in Caesar's dungeon, severely restricted in his actions. There were a multitude of things he could not do, be, or have.

[168] Jeremiah 12:23.

`Oh, don't you see, M. Poirot, it's all so difficult. It isn't
a question of David at all. It's me! I've changed. I've
been away for these three - four years. Now I've come
back I'm not the same person who went away. That's
the tragedy everywhere. People coming home changed,
having to readjust themselves. You can't go away and
lead a different kind of life and not change!'

`You are wrong,' said Poirot. `The tragedy of life is that
people do not change. '"[169]

On the strength of that observation, Poirot solved the crime and brought
a murderer to justice. Many other problems might be solved also, if
people would simply accept themselves as God has made them, and learn
how to draw strength rather than weakness from that fact. This
unchangeability may be a fact *of life, but, despite M. Poirot, it is only a*
tragedy *if you yourself make it so.*

Another example: I have a modest ability to play the piano, with a small
capacity to "play by ear" alone. I could with enormous effort improve
my musical skills a little. But I learnt years ago that no amount of
practice would ever turn me into a concert pianist. Marginal progress is
the best I could hope for. To endeavor even that much is hardly worth
the effort; to assay for higher accomplishment would be a mad courting
of humiliation and disappointment. And to think of myself as an artist,
or sculptor, or composer, or mathematician, or poet - and many other
things - would be even more laughable.

You too are circumscribed by similar boundaries.

But what is true of those skills is just as true of Christian ministry.
Whether it pleases us or not, proficiency in most areas of ministry will
always lie out of our reach. Most of us are fortunate if we reach a fair
level of skill in just one or two ways of serving God and the church. The
wise saint knows where his or her performance is poor, and cannot be
much improved, and so avoids those waiting snares of failure.

Must that induce a gloomy despondency? No; but it should create a
gracious humility, so that, as Paul said, *none of us think of ourselves*

[169] From Taken at the Flood; ch.12.

more highly than we ought to think, but assess ourselves soberly.[170] Here as in other matters of character, a pagan emperor showed greater wisdom than many Christians achieve -

> "You will never be remarkable for quick-wittedness. Be it so, then; yet there are still a host of other qualities (you could develop). Cultivate these, then, for they are wholly within your power: sincerity, for example, and dignity; industriousness, and sobriety. Avoid grumbling; be frugal, considerate, and frank; be temperate in manner and speech; carry yourself with authority. See how many qualities there are which could be yours at this moment... (You could have) remained chargeable with nothing worse than a certain slowness and dullness of comprehension - and even this you can correct with practice, so long as you do not make light of it or take pleasure in your own obtuseness."[171]

(III) WE ARE ALL LIMITED BY TWO THINGS

In his letter to the Romans (quoted just above), Paul said that two uncrossable walls surround each of us: our God-given *measure of faith;* and our God-given measure of grace". No one can prophesy, or serve, or teach, or do anything else in the church beyond the margins God has set. We should use each gift to the full measure in which it has been given;[172] but beyond that we cannot go, unless God himself chooses to enlarge his grace in us, and grant us a higher measure of faith.

Nothing in scripture requires any man or woman to do more than is allowed by the personal abilities and opportunities the Lord himself has placed in our reach. I used to cry out for God to make me into many things I thought I should be, but was not. Then I discovered that the Creator hardly needed me to tell him how he should have fashioned me. He had already crafted the man he wanted. Now my task was to develop that *man, not some mythical hero conjured up in my own imagination. It*

---

[170] Romans 12:3-6

[171] Marcus Aurelius in <u>Meditations</u> Bk 5, #5; op cit. Pg. 78. He is of course, admonishing himself.

[172] Remember in the parables of the <u>Talents</u> (Matthew 25:14-30), and of the <u>Pounds</u> (Luke 19:11-27).

was there is scripture all the time: whatever gift or calling we have, that is what we should commit ourselves to, not some personal daydream (see again Romans 12:6-8).

(IV) DON'T TAKE YOURSELF TOO SERIOUSLY

There is no more healthy quality than the ability to stand apart from yourself and laugh at your own pretensions. Pity those people who cannot chuckle at themselves, who view life with unyielding seriousness, who think themselves and their work are absolutely necessary. None of us are indispensable, and nothing we do, apart from God's grace, is worth anything. The world was made none the richer by our coming into it, and will be none the poorer for our leaving it.

> There was a water-drop, it joined the sea,
>
> A speck of dust, it was fused with the earth;
>
> What of your entering or leaving this world?
>
> A fly appeared, and disappeared![173]

Whatever you and I have done, or any of the greatest saints in history, God could have done just as well, or better, through another. He has never needed me. That he has allowed me to do a few small things for his kingdom is simply an expression of his kindness. I have not, and cannot, place him in my debt; he owes me nothing.

I have seen strong men collapse emotionally, or physically, or spiritually, under the demands of ministry. I have seen them sobbing like babies because everything suddenly seemed too much for them. I resolved that I would never allow myself to be trapped by Satan into such a delusion. Had those men been better able to keep things in their right perspective, to see the comical side of life, their ministry would never have been able to rob them of their joy and health.

> "A man must sometimes laugh at himself, or go mad.
> Few realize it. That is why there are so many madmen
> in the world."[174]

---

[173] The Ruba'iyat, quatrain 41; Avery & Heath-Stubbs; op. cit.

[174] One of the sayings of the fictional pirate, Peter (continued on next page)

We are all more ridiculous than we are wise, more fools than we are clever, more weak than we are strong. We are closer to clowns than we are to angels. So learn how to laugh at yourself. Nothing you and I do has in it more pathos than it has humor. Cultivate an eye for the comical. No one will ever have a nervous breakdown who can look at what he is doing, in all its pomp and solemnity, and giggle.

In an introduction to his poem The Contented Man, Robert Service refers to two unhappy friends of his, Saxon Dane, and McBean, and contrasts them with himself -

> "To how few is granted the privilege of doing work which lies closest to the heart, the work for which one is best fitted. The happy man is he who knows his limitations, yet bows to no false gods.
>
> McBean is not happy. He is overridden by his appetites, and to satisfy them he writes stuff that in his heart he despises.
>
> Saxon Dane is not happy. His dream exceeds his grasp. His twisted, tortured phrases mock the vague grandiosity of his visions.
>
> I am happy. My talent is proportioned to my ambition. ... I lack the divinity of discontent.
>
> True Contentment comes from within. It dominates circumstance. It is resignation added to philosophy, a Christian quality seldom attained except by the old."[175]

So be done with impossible dreams. Leave no space in your soul for illusions. Measure yourself with good-humoured honesty. Why wait until you get senile to get reasonable? Why go on living with pretence? Better we should cast aside our foolish pretences and learn the profound wisdom of Kahlil Gibran's saying: "Only the naked live in the sun."[176]

(continued from last page) Blood. From Captain Blood, by Rafael Sabatini, ch. 6.

[175] Ballads of a Bohemian; T. Fisher Unwin, London, 1921; pg. 127-128.

[176] The Gardens of the Prophet; Alfred A Knopf, New York, 1968; pg. 42.

156

Second: there is the responsibility of the church

Remember again my earlier analogy of a commercial corporation, and of the human body. Following those metaphors, surely the church will function best if each member is released to serve God in his or her special way. Why then do spiritual leaders keep on pressuring people to work in fields that are uncongenial to them? Why do they keep trying to make every saint a soul-winner, an intercessor, or a nurturer - and the like? The result of such harassment can hardly be other than frustration, pain, disappointment, fruitlessness.

One reason, I suppose, is that some pastors do not trust their people. They are sure that the people, if left to make their own choices, will choose wrongly. They fear to give the people any liberty, they dare not put any authority into the hands of the people. So they control, and dictate, and bully, holding tightly to the reins of command, ever anxious about a revolt. I prefer to think that the people of God, if given an opportunity to serve their Lord successfully will rush forward to seize it!

Another question: why do leaders commit the folly of beginning with programs instead of people? The pastor decides to set up, say, a young people's department. He announces his purpose, and then tries to enlist someone to run it, whether or not anyone in the church is truly called and skilled by God for that role.

What he should do is this. First determine that a young people's department is actually part of God's blueprint for his particular church. Perhaps it is; perhaps it is not. If it is, then the next step is not precipitously to set up the department. Instead, he should call the people to prayer, asking God to choose and send to them his appointed leader. Only when the right leader has been found should the program be inaugurated. Until then, do without a young people's ministry.

The same is true of any other activity: Sunday school; children's church; orchestra; choir; missions; men's and women's ministries; and so on.

Begin with people, not programs. Don't push people into artificially created programs; build programs around God-called, divinely-gifted people. If those people do not yet exist in the church then abandon the program. When you really need it, the Lord of the church will have the proper leaders ready for the job!

So the church has the major task of creating opportunities for each member to fulfil his or her calling. No one should be left fallow. Every gift should be identified and exploited for the glory of God. The success of the church is assured if all the people function within their "anointing". Nothing is so exhilarating as success, nor so motivating. Nothing is so debilitating, so dispiriting, as failure. Give people a job to do into which God has called them, for which they are gifted, and in which they know already they will surely succeed, and they will hardly have to be stirred to action. More likely the pastor will need to temper their zeal a little! But if a pastor prefers a congregation of guilt-stricken, burdened, despondent, and unfruitful misfits, then let him keep on conscripting them into various incongruous roles!

Let each of us, then, set ourselves to do well just what God has called us to do. Nothing more is asked of us in scripture.

Proposition four:

HARDSHIP –

"Put up with hardship"

Chapter Sixteen:

FINDING TRUE HAPPINESS

Consider this instruction, given by Sirach to his young disciple -

> "Do not ask the Lord to give you some high office, nor even the king to promote you... Do not yearn to be a judge, for you may not be strong enough to root out injustice; why risk being overawed by the powerful, and so ruin your integrity?"[177]

If you prefer something biblical, then listen to Solomon -

> *"Why do you wear yourself out trying to get rich? Have the good sense to stop now, for as soon as your eye is fixed on some treasure, away it will fly! All by itself your fortune will sprout wings and soar off like an eagle into the distant clouds... Just as it is foolish to eat too much honey, so you will find only sickness if you keep trying to pile honor on top of honor... You would do better to chase the wind than to toil hard for two handsful when you could hold one handful with peace of mind!"[178]*

Sage counsel! Let me paraphrase it a little: "Why do you wear yourself out trying to be successful? *No sooner have you won your prize than away it will fly!"[179]* Solomon means this: be cautious about hungering for position and power; be wary of preferment; don't be too anxious for success or honor. Promotion to a position above his capacity has destroyed many a good man. Are you sure you can handle the office you desire? You may be a fine shepherd of a flock of one hundred souls; but two hundred might break your spirit.

---

[177] Sirach 7:4-7

[178] Proverbs 23:4-5; 25:27; Ecclesiastes 4:6

[179] "Successful", of course, here means striving for success in a mere statistical sense; that is, someone yearning to gather a bigger crowd, or to earn more money, or to gain a higher position and the like. It does not refer to the "success" that every Christian must crave, of doing all that God wants, and of being all that God commands.

"We all dream of great deeds and high positions, away from the pettiness and humdrum of ordinary life. Yet success is not occupying a lofty place nor doing conspicuous work; *it is being the best that is in you.* Rattling around in too big a job is worse than filling a small one to overflowing.

"Dream, aspire by all means; but do not ruin the life you must lead by dreams of the one you would like to lead. Make the most of what you have and are. Perhaps your trivial immediate task is your sure way of proving your mettle. Do the thing near at hand, and great things may then come to your hand to be done.

If you can't be a highway then just be a trail,
If you can't be the sun be a star;
It isn't by size that you win or you fail -
Be the best of whatever you are!"[180]

Strangely, there are preachers who never doubt those propositions when they are applied to secular occupations, yet seem to think that they themselves are exempt. I feel the astonishment Omar Khayyam expressed in his wry quatrain -

Nobody has known anything better than sparkling wine
    Since the morning star and the moon graced the sky:
Wine-sellers astonish me because
    What can they buy better than what they sell?[181]

Is he talking only about wine, or perhaps rather about a deeper foible of humanity? At least we preachers should ask the poet's last question of ourselves: what can we buy better than what we sell? A man holds in his hand the sweet nectar of eternal life; he offers it to others, but himself drinks the sour vinegar of this world's vintage. His hearers press into the kingdom of God, while he is scrabbling for earthly plaudits; they reach for the treasures of heaven, while he craves the very material prosperity

---

[180] The Best-Loved Poems of the American People, selected by Hazel Felleman; Doubleday, New York, 1936; pg. 102-103; "Be The Best Of Whatever You are" by Douglas Malloch, stanza 4.

[181] The Ruba'iyat of Omar Khayyam; Peter Avery & John Heath-Stubbs; op.cit.; Stanza 110.

he once renounced. What an anomaly! The people abandon gain for the sake of godliness, while their pastor pursues godliness for the sake of gain![182]

The problem lies in the fault that occupied much of an earlier chapter: ambition masquerading as vision. *This is such a subtle delusion, and has snared so many, that I need to say a little more about it.*

> **Happiness ends where ambition begins!**

Edgar Allen Poe wrote a story, The Domain of Arnheim, which tells how a man named Ellison created a glorious garden that in some mystical way recaptured the ethereal beauty of Eden. During the story, Ellison declares his philosophy of life -

> "(Ellison) admitted but four elementary principles, or more strictly, conditions, of bliss. That which he considered chief was (strange to say!) the simple and purely physical one of free exercise in the open air. ... His second condition was the love of a woman. His third, and most difficult of realization, was the contempt of ambition. His fourth was an object of unceasing pursuit; and he held that, other things being equal, the extent of attainable happiness was in proportion to the spirituality of this object."

So according to Ellison there are four ingredients of happiness:

♦ *good health, based on physical exercise;*

♦ *the love of a godly spouse;*

♦ *the pursuit of a spiritual (not a material) goal; and*

♦ *the abjuring of ambition.*

The last one, said the philosopher, was the most difficult to realize!

Across the ages all the great moral thinkers (including the apostles) have reached the same conclusion. Despite the ubiquitous human addiction to

---

[182] 1 Timothy 6:5-10

success, they have echoed the words of Ellison: *"Happiness requires the renouncing of ambition."* An old English proverb expresses this even more pungently: *"Where ambition begins, there happiness ends; where ambition ends, there happiness begins!"*

An anonymous drama, Arden of Feversham (published in 1592), has a passage that describes the perils of aspiring to and achieving lofty office-

> "My golden time was when I had no gold;
> Though then I wanted, yet I slept secure;
> My daily toil begat me night's repose,
> My night's repose made daylight fresh to me.
> But since I climb'd the top bough of the tree
> And sought to build my nest among the clouds,
> Each gently breathing gale doth shake my bed,
> And makes me dread my downfall to the earth."[183]

Those who stand on the bottom step of life have at least this consolation: they are in no peril of falling! The poor fear no robber; the humble have no foe. Whatever can be taken from you is in the end no real wealth. Better to amass the invulnerable riches of godliness mixed with contentment (1 Timothy 6:6). "Uneasy lies the head that wears a crown,"[184] but those who have nothing to lose have nothing to dread. Sometimes God shows his fiercest anger, not by denying prayer, but by granting it -

> *"I wanted to feed you with the very finest wheat, and to satisfy you with the sweetest honey... But my people refused to listen to me, they weren't interested in what I wanted, so I gave them what their stubborn hearts craved, I condemned them to eat their own words."[185]*

This irony of providence - that answered prayer may be the worst form of divine punishment - has often been noted:

---

[183] Seneca: Four Tragedies; op. cit. Pg. 308-309. The passage is based on a discourse made by Thyestes to his son Tantalus, in Seneca's tragedy "Thyetes", lines 445 ff.

[184] Shakespeare Henry IV, part II.3.i.31.

[185] Psalm 81:16,11

"Granting our wishes is one of Fate's saddest jokes!...
Beware lest stern heaven hate you enough to hear your
prayers!... When the gods wish to punish us, they answer
our prayers"[186]

In similar vein an ancient poet encouraged even kings to be humble in
the face of changing fortune, and especially to tremble when they seem
most highly favoured by heaven -

"The King who rules with modest mien, of safety may be
sure.
The higher step of princely state that fortune hath us sign'd
The more behov'th a happy man humility of mind,
And dread the change that chance may bring, whose gifts so
soon be lost;
And chiefly then to fear the gods, while they thee favor
most!"[187]

So be wise, and temper ambition with humility, and especially with
contented submission to the Father's purpose, whether that means vast or
small accomplishment. This surely is the meaning of Solomon's
admonition -

*"Those who love money, will never be satisfied with
money, nor will they find any gain in their quest for
wealth."*[188]

Our eyes should be on the Lord, not some elusive earthly goal; he
himself should be our chief love, our true joy, the one passionate pursuit
of our life! Then let God do with us as he will, taking us to dizzying
heights of fame, or confining us to obscurity. So long as we gain his
approval, can anything else matter?

[186] J. R. Lowell (1819-1891); Anatole France (1881); Oscar Wilde (1895)

[187] From Seneca's tragedy "Troas", as translated by Jasper Heywood in 1559.
Watling, op. cit. Pg. 298

[188] Ecclesiastes 5:10

You began as dust, and you will end the same way

Sir Walter Raleigh is famed as the man who flung his cape into the mud for Queen Elizabeth to walk upon. He had cause to rue his vaunting ambitions, which began when he scratched a line of poetry on a palace window -

> The Queen and her court were gathered in the splendid gardens of the palace, and while they were thus engaged the Queen suddenly asked a lady, who was near her both in place and favor, what had become of the young squire who had so gallantly laid his cloak in the mud for her to walk upon.

> The Lady Paget answered, "She had seen Master Raleigh but two or three minutes since, standing at the window of a small pavilion or pleasure house, which looked out on the Thames, and writing on the glass with a diamond ring."

> "That ring," said the Queen, "was a small token I gave him to make amends for his spoiled mantle. Come Paget, let us see what he has made of it, for I can see through him already. He is a marvelously sharp-witted spirit."

> So they went to the spot, within sight of which, but at some distance, the young cavalier still lingered, as the fowler watches the net which he has set. The Queen approached the window on which Raleigh had used her gift to inscribe the following line -

> Fain would I climb, but that I fear to fall.

> The Queen smiled, read it twice over, once with deliberation, to Lady Paget, and once again to herself. "It is a pretty beginning," she said after the consideration of a moment or two; "but methinks the muse hath deserted the young wit at the very outset of his task. It were good-natured - were it not, Lady Paget - to

complete it for him?... Might not the answer (for fault of a better) run thus? -

If thy mind fails thee, do not climb at all. "

The dame of honor uttered an exclamation of joy and surprise at so happy a termination, while the Queen, thus encouraged, took off a diamond ring, and saying, "We will give this gallant some cause to marvel when he finds his couplet perfected without his own interference," she wrote her own line beneath that of Raleigh.

The Queen then left the pavilion, but Raleigh stole back to the window and read, with a feeling of intoxication, the encouragement thus given him by the Queen in person to follow out his ambitious career. His heart beat high with grateful pride, and with hope of future distinction.[189]

But Raleigh should have tempered his urge to "follow out his ambitious career". He incurred Elizabeth's displeasure, was gaoled by her in the Tower in 1592, and banished from the court for four years. A decade later, in 1603, he offended King James, who again imprisoned him - this time, for thirteen years. Stripped of all wealth and honours, locked in his cell, Raleigh gained a new perspective on life -

Give me my scallop shell of quiet,
My staff of faith to walk upon,
My scrip of joy, immortal diet,
My bottle of salvation,
My gown of glory, hope's true gage,
And thus I'll take my pilgrimage.

---

[189] From Kenilworth, by Sir Walter Scott, chapter seventeen; slightly modified. The story is based upon an actual incident that occurred in 1583. Charles Kingsley also, in his novel Westward Ho!, drew attention to Raleigh's Ambitions. He has Raleigh make his confession: "As for great purposes and lofty souls, who so fit to stand for them as I, being (unless my enemies and my conscience are liars both) as ambitious and as proud as Lucifer's own self!.. (Yet) I do but give you the world a fair challenge, and tell it, 'There – you know the worst of me; come and try a fall, for wither you or I must go down." (Op. cit., Ch. 9.)

Of death and judgment, heaven and hell,
Who oft doth think, must needs die well.[190]

Sadly, those sober reflections were not able to slay his craving for celebrity. After his release he determined again to try for the crown's favor. So he embarked on a treasure-hunting voyage to South America. Disaster overwhelmed him. His son was killed in a skirmish, he lost all his ships but one, most of his men perished, and he returned to England in disgrace. The king imprisoned him at once, and a few days later he was ignominiously beheaded. But the grace of God is limitless. In his final hours, as he prayed, a better perspective was again restored to Raleigh's mind. He composed the following lines and placed them in his Bible, where they were found after his death -

Even such is time, that takes in trust
Our youth, our joys, our all we have,
And pays us but with age and dust;
Who in the dark and silent grave,
When we have wandered all our ways,
Shuts up the story of our days.
And from which earth, and grave, and dust,
The Lord shall raise me up, I trust.

Those who are wise will not allow their highest hope to be located on this earth, where the wages in the end can never better "age and dust". Rather, they will fix their gaze upon possession of the City of God, which has eternal foundations.

---

[190] From the first and last stanza's of "The Passionate (continued on next page) (continued from last page) Man's Pilgrimage", written in prison in 1604

Chapter Seventeen:

PYRRHIC VICTORIES!

Look around you, in the world and in the church, and you will find countless examples of the misery that comes from misdirected ambition. What sorrow, what ruin, what pain has run rampant because priest and parishioner, prince and peasant, all refuse to take seriously the injunction, *"having food and raiment, therewith let us be content"!*[191]

Was Paul talking about everyone in the church, except its pastor? Is this something the preacher must preach to others, but is not obliged to do himself? Was the apostle thinking only about what we eat and wear; or was he expressing a philosophy of life that we should carry into every part of our existence - including Christian ministry? Are preachers alone allowed the privilege of discontent and restless ambition?

Somewhere years ago, I read a story about Pyrrhus, the renowned 3rd century B.C. King of Epirus, who came close to destroying the power of Rome. His victories, however, were immensely costly, so that when he was congratulated for one of them, Pyrrhus replied, *"Another such triumph and we are ruined!"*[192] He was eventually killed during a clash in the Greek town of Argos, by a woman who dropped a tile on him from a rooftop - an ignominious end for a daring and brilliant commander. Yet all his misfortunes could have been avoided had he listened to a friend. Before Pyrrhus embarked on his campaigns, a philosopher approached him (so it is said), and asked him what he was planning to do-

"I intend to make myself the master of all Greece," replied the king.
"And then?" asked the philosopher.
"Then I will bring Asia under my sceptre."
"And then?"

---

[191] 1 Timothy 6:8
[192] This, of course, is the origin of the proverbial expression "a pyrrhic victory" – that is, one so expensive it was hardly better than a defeat

"I will march my legions to Italy, and break the power of Rome."

"And then?"

"With the armies of nations under my command, Persia will be mine, and then Egypt, and I will rule the world!"

"And then?"

"Then I will go home, take my ease, and be content."

Upon which the philosopher, with some asperity, admonished the king: *"Why not go home now, take your ease, and be content?"*

Pyrrhus should have followed that sound advice! And there are pastors who should learn the same lesson. If you are one of them, may I urge you to be done with that gnawing hunger for bigness? Get rid of that sense of frustrated disappointment. Cast off the worldly yoke of carnal ambition, and learn to be content *where* you are, and with *who* you are, and with *what* you have. Ambition, especially when it is compulsive, and focused upon earthly achievement, is the ruin of godly contentment.

You are poor only if you think you are

"It is not the man who has too little, but the man who craves more, who is poor. ... True happiness comes from understanding your duty toward God and man, and from enjoying the present, without anxiously searching into the future... People who are neither elevated nor dejected by good or ill fortune possess an invincible greatness of mind. The wise man is content with his lot - whatever it may be - without restlessly yearning for what he lacks."[193]

Surely it is better to be happy in what you have than to grieve for what you have not. Would you really be any happier even if you were to gain the thing you crave - perhaps a bigger congregation, a finer building, a greater level of "success"? Consider those who already have what you

---

[193] Lucius Seneca, several of whose sayings I have already quoted in this book. After incurring the wrath of Nero and being condemned to death, he consoled his weeping family by urging them to accept with courage what they could not control. Forbidden by the emperor to make a will, he said he would leave his children the thing he had, the example of his life.

want - are they truly happy? Perhaps better contentment would come to you, not from gratifying your hunger, but from ridding yourself of it?

Have you ever met a discontented person whose pain did not come from trying to be what he is not, or do what he cannot, or seize what he has not? It is better to accept your limitations, to be humble about the insignificant place that even the greatest among us must occupy in the infinite panorama of the ages, than to be eaten up by fretful envies.

Measured against the limitless immensity of the universe, the difference between material failure and success in this world is absurdly unimportant -

"The Worldly Hope men set their Hearts upon
    Turns Ashes - or it prospers; and anon
Like Snow upon the Desert's dusty Face,
    Lighting a little hour or two - was gone."[194]

If the end result of worldly hope's realization or failure is no better than ashes or melted snow, what is there to choose between either state? We need a higher goal than one so earth-centred.

Epictetus, who was a slave in the palace of the grotesque Nero, once said-

"If a man is unhappy he is himself the sole cause of his misery, for God has made every person to be happy."

Could *you* display such equanimity?

If you were enslaved, and in the galling service of a despotic and barbarous maniac, could *you* keep such a mild temper? Yet Epictetus was a pagan, and we are Christians. He had only his philosophy to rest his soul upon; we have the authority of the gospel!

Consider also the wisdom of the great Preacher -

"Listen to the end of the matter; here is the complete picture. Reverence God, and obey his commandments. There is nothing more to be said. That is your whole

---

[194] The Ruba'iyat of Omar Khayyam; by Edward Fitzgerald, quatrain 17; Crown Publishers/Miller Graphics, 1979; pg. 28

duty. Except this: remember that everything you do, every hidden thought, whether good or evil, will be scrutinised by God on the day of Judgment!"[195]

| What you *are* is far more important than what you *do*. |

Surely the gospel firmly teaches this: what you are is far more important for true fulfillment than what you have or do? Everything else can be taken from you - fame, wealth, success, ministry, church, even the tomorrow from which you are hoping so much - but a godly character will stand imperishable for ever. If you cannot find contentment in yourself, and in Christ, it is crazy to seek it elsewhere.

So here is the path of wisdom: decide first who you would be - that is, what kind of Christian - and only then give thought to what you should do!

In one of his works, Christian Morals, the truly godly Sir Thomas Browne wrote -

> "Be substantially great in thyself, and more than thou appearest unto others; and let the World be deceived in thee, as they are in the Lights of Heaven. Hang early plummets upon the heels of Pride, and let Ambition have but an Epicycle and narrow circuit in thee. Measure not thyself by the morning shadow, but by the extent of thy grave, and reckon thyself above the earth by the line thou must be contented with under it. Spread not into boundless Expansions either of designs or desires.

> "Think not that mankind liveth but for a few, and that the rest are born but to serve those Ambitions, which make but flies of Men and wildernesses of whole Nations.

> If thou must needs rule (be content with) that Empire which every Man gives himself. He who is thus his own Monarch contentedly sways the sceptre of himself, not

---

[195] Ecclesiastes 12:13-14

envying the Glory of Crowned Heads and Elohims of the earth.[196]

"Could the World unite in the practice of that despised train of Virtues, which the Divine Ethicks of our Savior hath so inculcated upon us, the furious face of things must disappear, Eden would be yet to be found, and the Angels might look down, not with pity, but Joy upon us."[197]

What about a God-given vision?

Is there then no place for godly ambition, that is, for a true vision? Of course there is; but you need to keep it properly focused. Two great goals should motivate you -

♦ *first*: a heavenly aspiration, focused upon Christ[198]

♦ *second*: an earthly mandate, focused upon obedience[199]

That second goal is particularly important, for plainly, nothing else is incumbent upon us except to do the will of God. Hence this warning from the writings of the deeply godly J. R. Moseley

"Jesus gives to all of us who receive something of his nature a hatred for this love of money, power, and fame with which most of us have been tainted, and which has corrupted every priesthood thus far... (whether) Jewish, pagan, Catholic, (or) Protestant. We may give up these things slowly, but even to hate them in yourself more than in others is progress.

"The going of the Jesus way of limitless love and the hatred of things that hurt life, does not make us beggars,

---

[196] "Elohims"; that is "gods", rulers who carry on as though they were the Lord God (Elohim) himself

[197] Op. cit. Part One, section 19. Pg.424. In case you have forgotten, sir Thomas Browne (1605-82) was an English physician, author, and , pre-eminently, a Christian.

[198] Philippians 3:12-15.

[199] 2 Timothy 4:1,2,5.

but benefactors; does not make us paupers, but princes."[200]

And here is another salutary warning from a letter that Pope Gregory wrote in the year 601 to his missionary in England, the great Augustine, the first archbishop of Canterbury -

> "My very dear brother, I hear that Almighty God has worked great wonders through you for the nation which he has chosen. Therefore let your feeling be one of fearful joy and joyful fear at God's heavenly gifts - joy that the souls of the English are being drawn through outward miracles[201] to inward grace; fear lest the frail mind become proud because of these wonderful events. For when it receives public recognition, it is liable to fall through senseless conceit. We should remember how the disciples returned from their preaching full of joy, and said to their heavenly Master: *'Lord, even the devils are subject unto us, through thy name.'* But they received the prompt rejoinder: *'In this rejoice not. But rather rejoice because your names are written in heaven.'* For God's chosen do not all work miracles, yet the names of all are written in heaven. For those who are disciples of the truth should rejoice only in that good thing which they share with all men, and which they shall enjoy for ever. *"[202]*

Let that same good thing be the one unchanging source of all your joy. What else can you do? Would you fall into the snare that nearly ruined the psalmist, when he began to envy the prosperity of the ungodly? [203]Should we not rather echo the wisdom of Jeremiah, who said -

[200] Manifest Victory; Macalester Park Pub. Co., St Paul, MN; 1986; pg. 170

[201] A number of sick people had been healed through Augustine's ministry.

[202] From the Ecclesiastical History of the English People. Bk. 1, ch. 31, completed by the Venerable Bede in 731; rev. tr. By R. E. Latham; Penguin classics, London, 1990; pg. 93

[203] See Psalm 73:2-13.

"You have taught me, Lord, that no one can fix his own path through life; nor can we be sure that our plans will work out as we thought they would" (10:23).

So put your life in God's hand, and be content with his providence.

Chapter Eighteen:

PUT UP WITH HARDSHIP

You will never be ready to succeed without harm until you are willing to fail without despair!

Success, in statistical terms, is guaranteed to no-one in this world. Do you doubt that? Have you adopted the modern illusion that material prosperity is the unassailable right of every believer? Do you think God has promised you unfailing growth in your church, ever-increasing success in your ministry?

If so, perhaps you should ponder the wisdom of Solomon, while banishing from your mind the thought that these observations apply to everyone except yourself!

> *"After meditating on these things I finally concluded that God does hold in his hand the lives of all who are wise and righteous; yet not one of them knows whether tomorrow will bring love or hate!... I have also observed this happening under the sun: a swift man losing a race; a mighty man falling in battle. Then I saw hunger gripping a wise man, a clever man deprived of wealth, and the skillful stripped of honor. Time and chance happen to everyone, nor does anyone know when his hour will come. Like a fish caught in a net, like a bird trapped in a snare, so each person is surprised when sudden disaster strikes."*[204]

What a strange conclusion Solomon reached! He decided to accept two things that seem to contradict each other:

♦ *on one side, "God truly holds in his own hand the lives of the righteous;"*

♦ *on the other, "Not one of them knows whether tomorrow will bring love or hate!"*

[204] Ecclesiastes 9:1,11-12

Is there a quarrel between those ideas? No, for they express the mystery of life. Like you, I believe with all my heart that my days are in God's hand, and I always expect (and ask for) good things from him. Yet I cannot know what each hour will bring. Perhaps laughter, or tears; perhaps triumph, or tragedy.

"Time and chance," said Solomon, "happen to everyone." So much of what we call "success" depends upon being in the right place, or knowing the right person, at the right time! That is why God doesn't put much value on big achievement. Building a larger barn, erecting a higher tower, gathering a greater crowd, making a bigger fortune - none of that impresses God very much. Why should it? Measured against the stunning majesty and glory of his limitless universe, the finest human achievements hold as little significance as a falling leaf.

"Do sparks fly upward? So then are we born to trouble!"[205] Thus spoke the wise preacher, and who can deny the plain truth of his observation? Does this mean God has lost control? Of course not. But it does mean that ordinarily he chooses to work through the common vicissitudes of life in order to fulfil his great purpose.[206] The novelist Rafael Sabatini (perhaps unwittingly) simply echoed scripture when he wrote -

> "An intelligent observation of the facts of human existence will reveal to shallow-minded folk who sneer at the use of coincidence in the arts of fiction and drama, that life itself is little more than a series of coincidences. Open the history of the past at whatsoever page you will, and there you shall find coincidence at work bringing about events that the merest chance might have averted. Indeed, coincidence may be defined as the very tool used by Fate to shape the destinies of men and nations."[207]

---

[205] Job 5:7

[206] Romans 8:28

[207] Captain Blood; Ch. 18.

You may prefer to replace "coincidence" with "Providence", but the result is the same: there is a seeming capriciousness about life that for all of us clouds each new day with dark uncertainty.[208]

Born to Trouble

Once, while watching a classical music program on television, I heard these words: *"You can't predict the course of your career, no matter how talented you are. So much depends on luck!"* The speaker was Maestro Michael Tilson, guest conductor of the New World Symphony of Miami. He was addressing a group of highly skilled young musicians, who were all dreaming of gaining renown in the world of music. The maestro knew that neither talent alone, nor hard work, would bring those young people to the realization of their dreams. Some of the less skilled would gain top positions in their profession; others more talented would fail. Beyond toil or talent, their future depended upon a conjunction of things over which they had little control.

But he said nothing more than Solomon had declared long before -

> *"When everything is going well, you should be happy; but it may just as well go wrong. If it does, then remember this: God has put prosperity and ruin alongside each other in a way that stops all of us from predicting the future. Look around you! How can you fail to see that sometimes good people get what belongs to the wicked, and sometimes wicked people get what belongs to the good.*[209]

For any of us, life can be erratic! If you still doubt that, just look around you! Search church history. Think about the mixed fortunes of the ancient kings of Israel and Judah. Some wicked monarchs enjoyed long, peaceful, and prosperous reigns, while some godly rulers after many wars and troubles were cut off in the prime of life.

Another way to look at it is this: recognise the distinction between the general promise of prosperity to the people of God as a whole, and the diverse ways in which that promise may be worked out for individuals.

---

[208]   James 4:13-16

[209]   Ecclesiastes

Think about this for a moment: the Lord promised Israel that its army would enjoy great success in war; nonetheless, any of the soldiers might lose his life in battle; none of them had any guarantee that they could emerge from the fight unscathed.[210]

So the question is not how well you prosper in your work, which may be taken out of your hands by some vicissitude of health, fortune, or circumstance. The real issue is how well you succeed as a *Christian*. How do you handle the ups and downs of life? Do they make you or break you?

> "King Arthur had been soundly defeated in personal combat with the Knight of the Fountain, Pellinore. He was angry, ashamed, and weaponless, and he complained bitterly to Merlin: `You must be proud to serve me, a defeated king... What is a knight without a sword? A nothing - even less than a nothing.'
>
> "`It is a child speaking,' said Merlin, `not a king, and not a knight, but a hurt and angry child, or you would know, my lord, that there is more to a king than a crown, and far more to a knight than a sword.'
>
> "`But Pellinore defeated me,' lamented Arthur.
>
> "`Somewhere in this world,' said Merlin, `there is defeat for everyone. Some are destroyed by defeat, and some are made small and mean by victory. Greatness lies in one who triumphs equally over defeat and victory.'"[211]

But surely there is some way to predict whether one's life will be prosperous or poverty-stricken, triumphant or shattered? Surely good things happen to good people, and bad things to the wicked? Doesn't scripture itself say that

> *"No harm will touch the righteous, but watch the wicked get their fill of adversity! Nothing but ill fortune dogs the*

---

[210] See, for example, Deuteronomy 20:3-7.

[211] Adapted from John Stienbeck op. cit. Pg. 57,58

feet of sinners, while the righteous are rewarded with bountiful blessings!"[212]

That may often be the truth of the matter, and in an ultimate, eternal sense, it is always true. But in this life a thousand changes of fortune may bring happiness to the ungodly and tears to the godly. Augustine, bishop of Hippo, understood this fifteen hundred years ago -

---

Who knows what tomorrow will bring?

"In our present situation we are learning to bear with equanimity the ills that even good men suffer,[213] and at the same time not to set much store by the good things which the wicked also acquire. In this way there is salutary instruction from God, even in situations where God's justice is not apparent. For we do not know by what decision of God this good man is poor, while that wicked man is rich; why this man is cheerful, though, in our opinion, his desperate moral character makes him deserve the tortures of grief, while that man, whose exemplary life convinces us that he deserves to be cheerful, is full of sorrow; why an innocent man leaves the   court   not   merely   un-avenged   but   actually condemned, ... while, in contrast, his criminal adversary gloats over him, as he goes away not only unpunished but even vindicated; why the impious man is hale and hearty, while the devout man pines away in weakness;

---

[212]   Proverbs 12:21; 13:21.

[213]   Just before Augustine wrote these words the horrifying news had swept the world that mighty Rome, which had stood inviolate for a thousand years, had been taken and plundered by barbarians. Wherever the invaders marched, Christian churches were destroyed, the clergy were carried off into slavery, maidens were raped, houses were burned - a swathe of devastation and terror. To the people of that time, it seemed as though the world was coming to an end, law and order were devoured, the very fabric of the greatest civilisation mankind had ever seen was being torn to shreds. Augustine himself, just before his death, endured the horror of his own beloved city crumbling beneath an assault by the Vandals. He died before the city was taken, so was spared the anguish of watching the churches and people he had nurtured so faithfully being ravaged by the cruel foe.

> why young men practice highway robbery, and enjoy
> excellent health, while infants who could not have hurt
> anyone, even by a word, are afflicted by all manner of
> cruel diseases; ... one whose record is full of crimes is
> exalted to high position, while another who is beyond
> reproach is hidden in the shadows of obscurity. Who
> could list or enumerate all the other examples of this
> kind?" [214]

All this would be more comprehensible, Augustine goes on to say, if
only there were some visible consistency in divine providence; that is, if
the wicked always received good things in life, while the righteous knew
nothing but sorrow. At least it could then be argued that God is showing
mercy to the unrighteous simply to bring them to repentance; but if not,
then to compensate them for the eternal miseries to come. Of the
righteous it could be said that God is training them through hardship to
inherit the full glory of his coming kingdom.

Or, perhaps the reverse: if the righteous received only good, and the
unrighteous only evil, then it could be said that God's moral order is
being clearly vindicated. That, of course, was the way Job's friends
wanted to see the world - except that the patriarch's experience gave
them the lie. Despite our craving for a simple, uncluttered, black and
white world, life remains complex and uncertain, full of inequity and
injustice. What you have today, you may lose tomorrow; what you lack
today, you may gain tomorrow; the sun rises and it also sets; the tides of
life flow in and out; seasons come and go. A man can rise from prison to
the throne, and then fall back again into poverty. As Solomon said, "I
have seen slaves in splendor on horseback, and princes walking on foot
like slaves." How unpredictable life is! The [215]sensible know it, and
echo the wisdom of the philosopher"

> In beating down what war hath won, by proof I have been
> taught,
> What pomp and pride in wink of eye, may fall and come to
> naught.

---

[214] <u>City of God</u> Bk. 20, ch. 2; tr. by Henry Bettenson; Penguin Books, London; 1977; pg. 896,897.

[215] Ecclesiastes 4:14; 6:1,2; 10:7.

Troy made me fierce and proud of mind, Troy makes me 'f
raid withal:
The Greeks now stand where Troy late fell;
Each thing may have his fall!" [216]

In the same drama there is a place where the chorus raises a lament,
expressing bewilderment at the apparent caprice of life. The heavenly
bodies continue their stately and regular procession across the sky; the
seasons follow each other in unvarying rhythm; the laws of nature seem
immutable and wholly dependable. Why then is human life so turbulent
and precarious?

"But why art Thou that all dost guide,
    between whose hand the pole doth sway,
And at whose will the Orbs do slide,
    careless of man's estate alway?
Regarding not the good man's case,
    not caring how to hurt the ill.
Chance beareth rule in every place,
    and turneth man's estate at will;
She gives the wrong the upper hand,
    the better part she doth oppress;
She makes the highest low to stand,
    her Kingdom all is orderless." [217]

On being content to be a slave

So while it may be generally true that crime doesn't pay, and that a godly
life usually brings great benefit, the exceptions are many. We are driven
to conclude with Augustine: "the judgments of God become the more
inscrutable, and his ways the more intractable!" But since we have little
say or choice in the matter, we might as well accept without complaint
the seemingly capricious inequalities, the arbitrary fluctuations of
fortune, that abound everywhere. By all means change what you can, as
Paul advised Christian slaves -

---

[216] From Jasper Heywood's 1559 translation of Seneca's tragedy "Troas";
Watling, op. cit. pg 298.

[217] Ibid. pg. 299-300. (Lines 814-823 of Heywood's drama.)

*"Were you a slave when Christ called you to himself?
That is nothing to be ashamed of - but if you are able to
gain your freedom, then you should do so. ... Each one of
you, dear friends, as those who are answerable only to
God, should be content in whatever situation God has
seen fit to place you"* [218]

But where a situation or environment cannot be changed, then don't
resent it, but rather grip it in faith and turn it into a stairway to paradise!
That at least was the counsel of the remarkable Sir Thomas Browne -

"Since the Stars of Heaven do differ in glory; ... since
there are some Stars so bright that they can hardly be
looked on, some so dim that they can scarce be seen, and
vast numbers not to be seen at all even by Artificial
Eyes; Read thou the Earth in Heaven, and things below
from above. Look contentedly upon the scattered
differences of things, and expect not equality in lustre,
dignity, or perfection, in Regions or Persons below;
where numerous numbers must be content to stand like
(the stars in a misty nebula), little taken notice of, or dim
in their generations. ... (Wait patiently for) the World to
come, when the last may be the first and the first the last;
when Lazarus may sit above Caesar, and the just obscure
on Earth shall shine like the Sun in Heaven; when
personations shall cease, and Histrionics of happiness be

---

[218] 1 Corinthians 7:17-24. Notice however that some translations make Paul say
that even if a slave <u>could</u> gain his freedom, he should refuse it, so that he
might better follow the example of Christ, who made himself a slave for us.
They claim that Paul wrote: Even if a chance for escape from slavery should
come, why would you want to take it? if Christ called you while you were a
slave, have you not become his freedman? And if Christ called you while
you were free, have you not become his slave? You are all in the service of
Christ.'

How utterly foreign that is to our way of thinking! 'What? He should not seize
the chance to shake off his chains, and go out and win a multitude of souls,
and build a huge church? How outrageous!' But Paul, I think, had a value
system far distant from ours.

over; when Reality shall rule, and shall be as they shall be for ever." [219]

A whining saint is an unpleasant thing

How offensive it is to hear a Christian, who should already be half living in heaven, whining because events have turned out unpleasantly on earth! Life is not fair, and never has been. It was not fair to Jesus, and we are not above our Master. How refreshing it is to turn away from the petulant complaints of the self-indulgent, the ambitious, and the dissatisfied. Listen to these words of the writer of a great Letter to the Romans - not Paul, but Ignatius.[220] He was in fetters at the time, being carried off to die at Rome. He had refused to burn incense to Caesar, and so had been condemned to be thrown to the lions. The journey to his terrible death took many weeks, and on the way he wrote to seven churches. Among them was a letter to Rome, telling them of his coming, and begging them to make no attempt to postpone or cancel his martyrdom

> "All the way from Syria to Rome I have been chained to a detachment of soldiers who have behaved like animals towards me. I tried giving them money, but the more I gave them the more roughly they treated me. Quite honestly, they are like a pack of leopards, enjoying their role as hunters, with me as their prey. Well, that has some advantages. I may as well get used to leopards' now - it will be lions, and real ones at that, when I get to Rome. So I can now make some progress towards preparing myself spiritually and mentally for what lies ahead. All I pray is that when the moment comes the lions will be quick about it

> "Forgive me for writing like this, but I do know what is best for me. No power, human or spiritual, must hinder my coming to Jesus Christ. So whether the way be fire,

---

[219] Op. cit. Part 111.14.

[220] Fl. circa 35?-107? He was a disciple of the apostle John, and became bishop of Antioch in Syria. The passage is quoted in Christian Classics, ed. Veronica Zundel; Eerdmans Pub. Co., Grand Rapids; 1985;

or crucifixion, or wild beasts in the arena, or the mangling of my whole body (by torture), I can bear it, provided I am assured it is the way to him

"So far as I concerned, to die in Jesus Christ is better than to be king of the whole wide world!"

Has that martyr's heart gone from the church? If it has, we no longer deserve the name "Christian".

Ponder rather the mystery of goodness

Modern life protects us from the countless sorrows and perils that beset our forefathers, so that we are stunned when any misfortune strikes at us. Hence we tend to be much distressed by the mystery of pain. We demand to know the cause of the world's misery. We insist on answers, and we want them simple. God forbid that we should be confronted by a swirling fog of enigma! The idea of being content to look through a "dark glass" may have been adequate for Paul. It will not suit modern proponents of hyper-faith, who refuse to entertain any doubt about their right to unsullied happiness and flawless success.

But those who have suffered, yet refused to capitulate to pain, tend to ask a different question. They do not cry, "Solve for me the mystery of pain!" Rather, they demand, "Explain to me the mystery of joy?" If we can discover the source of love and laughter, of melody and life, then perhaps we might also learn the secret of pain and tears, of tragedy and ruin.

Let me refer again to that irenic, gracious, and urbane physician, Sir Thomas Browne. He had to live through the anguish of the death of eight of his twelve children, yet his writings sparkle with gentle humour, kindly sympathy, and grace. He steadily maintained that Christ like character until his death in 1682, at 77 years of age. Commenting on this remarkable life, one of his modern editors, C. A. Patrides writes -

> "Browne had seen the devil at high noon and averted his gaze, because as he trusted that the worst might turn to laughter. We protest, because such a vision appears to negate reality. But where we might be obsessed with the problem of evil and pain, Sir Thomas Browne explored

with eager thought the equally complex problem of the existence of goodness and joy." [221]

And Sir Thomas himself said - [222]

> '... when I survey the occurrences of my life, and call into account the finger of God, I can perceive nothing but an abyss and masse of mercies, either in general to mankind, or in particular to my selfe; and whether out of the prejudice of my affection, or an inverting and partial conceit of his mercies, I know not, but those which others terme crosses, afflictions, judgements, misfortunes, to me who enquire farther into them than their visible effects, they both appeare, and in event have ever proved the secret and dissembled favours of his affection...

> "(Therefore) what a frensie were it to terme (these things) a punishment, rather than an extremity of mercy, and to groane under the rod of his judgements, rather than admire the Scepter of his mercies? Therefore to adore, honour, and admire him is a debt of gratitude due from the obligation of our nature, states, and conditions; and with these thoughts, he knows them best, will not deny that I adore him;..."

---

[221] Op. cit., 'Introduction' pg. 52

[222] Religio Medici Part One, Sec. 53. Op. cit. pg. 126,127. It is a pity that the chauvinism of the 17th century prevents us from knowing much about Browne's wife, Dorothy Mileham. She, after all, was the patient and sorrow-wracked bearer of those twelve children. Perhaps she had much to do with shaping her husband's saintliness. They were married for 41 years. She survived Browne's death by two years.

Epilogue:

OUR HIGHEST DUTY

The highest duty of every Christian is to adore God, and to serve only him through Christ, until life ends. If you hold to that view, you will never allow unexpected misfortune to crush you, nor permit bitterness to find lodging in your spirit. Should you fail in this, even the pagan philosopher-king will rise against you on the day of judgment -

> "Be like the headland against which the waves break and break: it stands firm, until presently the watery tumult around it subsides once more to rest. `How unlucky I am, that this should happen to me!' By no means; say rather, `How lucky I am, that it has left me with no bitterness; unshaken by the present, and undismayed by the future.' The thing could have happened to anyone, but not everyone would have emerged unembittered. ...
>
> "Does this thing which has happened hinder you from being just, magnanimous, temperate, judicious, discreet, truthful, self-respecting, independent...?
>
> "So here is a rule to remember in the future, when anything tempts you to feel bitter: Not, `This is a misfortune,' but, `To bear this worthily is good fortune.'"[223]

Nothing therefore is a misfortune unless the recipient thinks it is. For a Christian, true misfortune exists only in a readiness to become vexed and yield to complaint. The worst disaster that can happen to me is to reckon anything that does happen to be a disaster! Instead, I should see each event as another step closer to heaven. If I love God, if I am obedient to his call, then his divine grace imparts to every happening a redemptive quality.

---

[223] Marcus Aurelius, <u>Meditations</u> Bk 4, #49. Op.cit. pg. 75

Nothing can finally destroy me unless I allow it to do so. Everything can be turned into an ascent to Paradise.[224]

> "When darkness is upon you, say: `This darkness is dawn not yet born; and though night's travail be full upon me, yet shall dawn be born unto me even as unto the hills."[225]

Those who are wise remember they are mortal

On his Sixth Voyage, Sinbad the Sailor visited a strange land called Sarandib. After returning safely to Baghdad he recounted his adventures to the great Caliph, and described the King of Sarandib -

> "... the King's seat of State is in a splendid throne placed upon a gigantic elephant with his courtiers and officials standing about him on a highly decorated platform... (There) are around His Majesty a thousand other elephants upon which sit the princes of the land; and, surrounding all, on every hand, ten thousand horsemen clad in silk and gold...

> "(A) crier goes always before the King, exalting him to heaven, while another goes behind him proclaiming, `He is indeed great, yet he will die! Again I say it, and again, and again, he will surely die!'"[226]

If nothing else will suffice to keep us humble, and to cast the events of this world into a small perspective, then surely the recollection of our mortality, and of eternity to follow, will do so! What are we but dust turning into dust? And even that is not wholly our own -

> When your dear soul and mine have left the body,
> They will set on our grave two tiles;
> And then, for the tiles on others' graves,
> They will set your dust and mine in a mould.

---

[224] Romans 8:28
[225] Kahil Gibran, The Garden of the Prophet, pg. 32
[226] From a child's book, now lost

Every particle of dust on a patch of earth
Was a sun-cheek or brow of the morning star;
Shake the dust off your sleeve carefully -
That too was a delicate, fair face.

Oh wise elder, get up earlier in the morning;
Look closely at that boy sifting dust;
Advise him, `Gently, gently sift
The brains of Kaikobad and eyes of Parviz.'[227]

Life is so short, the endless ages so long, it is a kind of insanity to have more cognisance of this world than of that.

What is fame here worth, in comparison with renown there? Which is more to be desired, the plaudits of men or of angels, the praise of the crowd or of the Lord?

Life has always been unfair

Have you ever wondered what Mrs James might have thought about the way Peter was supernaturally rescued from prison by an angel, while her husband, despite the equally fervent prayers of the saints, was beheaded?[228]

Imagine how she felt when Mrs Peter stood up in church to tell with great joy how wonderfully God had heard her prayers, and what a miracle the Lord had wrought. I wonder if Mrs James stole away to weep in lonely despair, *"Why, Lord; why, why, why?"*

Then, what would you say to the families of the guards, who had nothing to do with Peter's escape, yet were harshly put to death by Herod? Scant justice was offered to them, nor even any opportunity to repent, let alone to serve God in response to the miracle they had unwittingly shared.

---

[227] The Ruba'iyat of Omar Khayyam, stanza, 57-59; Avery, op. cit. Pg. 60, 61. Kaikobad and Parvis were two Muslim heroes, the first legendary, the second a Persian king of the late 6th century.

[228] Acts 12:1-19

Or again, consider Paul, who was once released from prison by an earthquake, while he and Silas were singing God's praises at midnight.[229]

But did that ever happen again. No; only once was he so favored! Perhaps he sang midnight hymns on the other occasions he was imprisoned, hoping for a similar miracle? We don't know; but it wouldn't have changed anything. Did Paul expect another earthquake? If so, he expected in vain. During all his other imprisonments he had to wait on Caesar's good pleasure, for God chose not to intervene.

Whatever their immediate reaction to life's vicissitudes might have been, all those biblical characters sooner or later had to find a place of repose in the providence of God. They couldn't change the state in which they found themselves. All the victory they would ever know had to be found and expressed right there.

Where then does "mountain-moving" faith have a place? Surely, to seize whatever God has truly promised, and to enable us to fulfil all that he has called us to be and to do. But this must also be faced: faith is not a medium of infallible success, but rather of loyal and trusting obedience to God, whether that brings poverty or plenty, peace or pain, success or failure[230]-

> "Read (Hebrews 11:32-39a). The author lists men and women who have had great victory through faith. Then, without skipping a beat, he mentions people who were tortured, persecuted, killed. They had faith too. Faith isn't what rescues you. It's what guides you. It may guide you to the cross, or it may guide you to victory. You don't know. If you knew, it wouldn't be faith. Risks are not to be evaluated in terms of the probability of success, but in terms of the value of the goal."[231]

Does that mean we should never try a great venture?

Of course not!

---

[229] Acts 16:24-26

[230] Philippians 4:11-13; Hebrews 11:32-39a

[231] Ralph Winter, missiologist, in "Christianity Today", Sep 7, 1984

Dream as expansively as you can, attempt the noblest deeds you can aspire to, expect marvelous things from God. Be optimistic! Yet keep a realistic outlook on life. Perhaps everything will work out better than you had ever hoped or dared to dream; but in the end, you cannot know what tomorrow holds.[232]

So there is a nice balance to be maintained between hope of great things and compliance with reality. The 19th century English poet, Matthew Arnold, caught this balance finely in the last stanza of his poem, *Empedocles on Etna* -

> I say, Fear not! Life still
>> Leaves human effort scope!
> But, since life teems with ill,
>> Nurse no extravagant hope.
> Because thou must not dream, thou
>> need'st not then despair.

That is a nice phrase: "nurse no extravagant hope." Keep everything in balance. Remember the biblical ideal of *"moderation in all things"*, neither being too aggressive nor too passive, neither expecting too much nor too little, but content to do what the Lord appoints, and to leave the result in his hand.[233]

How fine it would be if after your death a biographer would say of you as the Venerable Bede said of Saint Aidan -

> "He cultivated peace and love, purity and humility; he set himself to keep as well as to teach the laws of God, and was diligent in study and prayer. He used his priestly authority to check the proud and powerful; he tenderly comforted the sick; he relieved and protected the poor.

> "To sum up in brief what I have learned from those who knew him, he took pains never to neglect anything that he had learned from the writings of the evangelists and prophets, and he set himself to carry them out with all his powers. I greatly

---

[232] James 4:13-15.

[233] Philippians 4:5

admire and love all these things about Aidan, because I have no doubt that they are pleasing to God."[234]

The Last Word

"Of the writing of many books, there is no end," said the Preacher[235] One reason for this is because no single author ever sees the whole truth of a matter. So one book inescapably provokes another, either in rebuttal or complement. No doubt that will be the fate of this volume. Some readers will react to it with passion, and feel the need to correct what he or she deems to be my faults. I encourage you to read their books as well as mine. If possible, I will read them myself. So we will advance together toward the perfection of the Father's will.

---

[234] Op. cit. Bk. III.17; pg. 170. Aiden, died in 651, he was bishop and friend to King Oswold of Northumbria, in central Britain. He could have been rich and powerful; but he preferred poverty and separation from courtly affairs, which kept him free to rebuke when necessary even the wealthy and the mighty

[235] Ecclesiastes 12:13.

BIBLIOGRAPHY

Acts of King Arthur and His Noble Knights, The; John Steinbeck, Heineman, London, 1976.

Anti-Nicene Fathers; tr. by A. Cleveland Coxe; 19th century work; reprint by EerdmansPub. Co. 1978.

Art of Understanding Yourself, The; C. G. Osborne; Zondervan Publishing House; Grand Rapids, 1973.

Ballads of a Bohemian; T. Fisher Unwin; London, 1921.

Behind the Curtain, E. D. Biggers; Bantam Books; New York, 1974.

Best-Loved Poems of the American People, The; selected by Hazel Felleman; Doubleday; New York, 1936.

Captain Blood; Rafael Sabatini.

Christian Century Magazine; April 10, 1991.

Christian Classics; ed. Veronica Zundel; Eerdman's Pub. Co., Grand Rapids, 1985.

Church, The; Barry Chant; Vision Publishing; Australia.

Context, newsletter; March 15, 1988.

Early Christian Writings; The Didache; tr. Maxwell Staniforth; Penguin Books, 1968.

Essays: First Series; Self Reliance; Ralph Waldo Emerson (1841).

Faith Dynamics; Ken Chant; Vision Publishing; Australia.

Gardens of the Prophet, The; Khalil Gibrand; Alfred A Knopf; New York, 1968.

Henry IV; William Shakespeare.

History of Christianity; A; K.S. Latourette; Harper & Row; New York, 1975.

<u>History of the Expansion of Christianity, A</u>; Zondervan Publishing House; Grand Rapids, Michigan, 1970.

<u>Kenilworth</u>; Sir Walter Scott.

<u>Major Works, The</u>; Christian Morals; Sir Thomas Browne; ed. C. A. Patride.

<u>Meditations</u>; Marcus Aurelius; tr. Maxwell Staniforth; Penguin Books; 1986.

<u>Mountain Movers</u>; Ken Chant; Vision Publishing; Australia,

<u>Passionate Man's Pilgrimage, The</u>; Sir Walter Raleigh; 1604.

<u>Pensées</u>; tr. John Warrington; J. M. Dent & Sons Ltd., London, 1973.

<u>Pillow book of Sei Shonagon, The</u>; tr. Ivan Morris; Penguin Classics; London, 1967.

<u>Practice of the Presence of God, The</u>; Brother Lawrence; Burns & Oates; London, 1977.

<u>Prophet, The</u>; Kahlil Gibran; Alfred A. Knopf; New York, 1968.

<u>Renegade, The</u>; Cherry Tree Books; London, 1937.

<u>Royal Priesthood; Ken Chant; Vision Publishing; Australia.</u>

<u>Ruba'iyat of Omar Khayyam, The</u>; tr. Peter Avery & John Heath-Stubbs; Penguin Classics; London, 1983.

<u>Seneca's Four Tragedies and Octavia</u>; tr. E.F. Watling; Penguin Classics; 1970.

<u>Throne Rights</u>; Ken Chant; Vision Publishing; Australia.

<u>Walden</u>; Henry David Thoreau; 1854.

<u>Westward Ho</u>; Charles Kingsley; Collins Clear Type Press; London.

<u>What Luther Says</u>; compiled by Ewald M Plass; Concordia Publishing House; Missouri, 1959.

<u>Worthies of England, The</u>; (1662); Thomas Fuller; ed. by Richard Barber; The Folio society; London 1987.

www.ingramcontent.com/pod-product-compliance
Lightning Source LLC
Chambersburg PA
CBHW060741100426

42813CB00027B/3015